Architecture and Disjunction

Bernard Tschumi

Architecture and **Disjunction**

The MIT Press   Cambridge, Massachusetts   London, England

This book was set in Trump by DEKR Corporation and was printed and bound in the United States of America.

Library of Congress Cataloging-in-Publication Data

Tschumi, Bernard, 1944–

    Architecture and disjunction / Bernard Tschumi.

    p. cm.

    Includes bibliographical references.

    ISBN 0-262-20094-5

    1. Architecture and society—History—20th century. 2. Joint occupancy of buildings. 3. Architecture—Technological innovations. I. Title.

NA2543.S6T78 1994

720'.1'0309048—dc20

93-45683

CIP

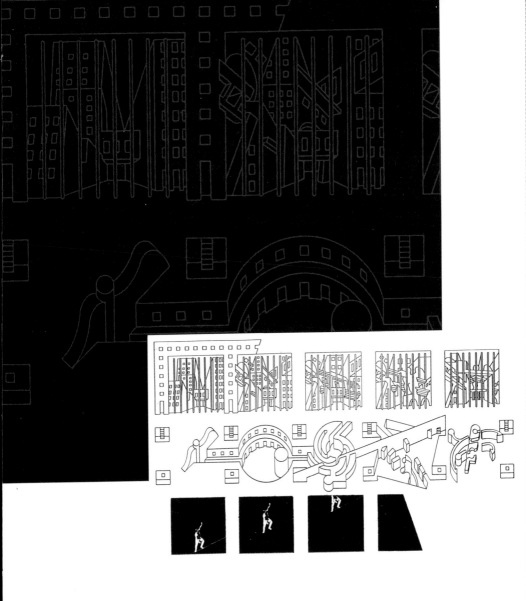

Bernard Tschumi, from *The Manhattan Transcripts,* 1977–1981.

Contents

Sources and Acknowledgments

"The Architectural Paradox" and "Questions of Space" originally appeared in a different form as "Questions of Space: The Pyramid and the Labyrinth (or the Architectural Paradox)" in *Studio International*, September–October 1975. Reprinted by permission of the Medical Tribune Group, London.

"The Pleasure of Architecture" originally appeared in a different form in *AD* (*Architectural Design*), March 1977. It is reprinted by permission of the Academy Group Limited, London.

"Space and Events" originally appeared in a different form in *Themes III: The Discourse of Events* (London: Architectural Association, 1983), and is reprinted by permission.

"Architecture and Transgression" originally appeared in *Oppositions 7*, Winter 1976 (Cambridge: The MIT Press), and is reprinted by permission.

"Architecture and Limits I, II, and III" originally appeared in *Artforum* in December 1980, March 1981, and September 1981, respectively; "Violence of Architecture" appeared in September 1981. All are reprinted by permission of Artforum International.

"Sequences" originally appeared in *The Princeton Journal: Thematic Studies in Architecture*, vol. 1, 1983. Reprinted by permission of The Princeton Journal and Princeton Architectural Press.

"Madness and the Combinative" originally appeared in *Precis*, 1984 (New York: Columbia University Press), and is reprinted by permission.

"Abstract Mediation and Strategy" originally appeared in a different form in Bernard Tschumi, *Cinégramme Folie: Le Parc de la Villette* (New York: Princeton Architectural Press, 1987), and is reprinted by permission.

"Disjunctions" is reprinted by permission from *Perspecta 23: The Yale Architectural Journal*, January 1987.

"De-, Dis-, Ex-" originally appeared in Barbara Kruger and Phil Mariani, eds., *Remaking History* (Seattle: Bay Press, 1989) and is reprinted with permission of Bay Press.

Architecture and Disjunction ▬

Introduction ▬

disjunction: the act of disjoining or condition of being disjoined;
separation, disunion. The relation of the terms of a disjunctive
proposition. *fr* dissociation.

—Webster's Dictionary

Running through the essays collected in this book is a relentless affirmation: that there is no architecture without
program, without action, without event. As a whole, these
texts reiterate that architecture is never autonomous, never
pure form, and, similarly, that architecture is not a matter of
style and cannot be reduced to a language. Opposing an over-
rated notion of architectural form, they aim to reinstate the
term *function* and, more particularly, to reinscribe the movement of bodies in space, together with the actions and events

that take place within the social and political realm of architecture. But these texts refuse the simplistic relation by
which form follows function, or use, or socioeconomics. In
contrast, they argue that in contemporary urban society, any
cause-and-effect relationship between form, use, function,
and socioeconomic structure has become both impossible
and obsolete.

Written between 1975 and 1991, these essays
were conceived as successive chapters of a book that could—
somewhat in the manner of Le Corbusier's *Vers une Architecture* and Robert Venturi's *Complexity and Contradiction
in Architecture*—provide a description of our architectural
condition at the end of the twentieth century. While their
common starting point is today's disjunction between use,
form, and social values, they argue that this condition, instead of being a pejorative one, is highly "architectural."
Throughout the following chapters, architecture is defined
as the pleasurable and sometimes violent confrontation of
spaces and activities. The first group of texts, assembled
under the theme of Space, analyzes earlier theories of architectural space and suggests that a precise definition will
always include mutually exclusive or contradictory terms.
Such an opposition introduces the notion of architectural
pleasure as the experience of space intersects with its more
conceptual aspects. The second part, entitled Program, begins by questioning the three classical tenets of beauty, solidity, and utility, and suggests that the programmatic
dimension of usefulness be expanded into the notion of
event. "Violence of Architecture" provides a key account of

the rich and complex relations between spaces and the events that occur within them. The third part, Disjunction, develops the implications of the first two parts. Often related to the beginnings of an architectural practice that tried to expand these concepts in the form of actual buildings, it tries to propose a new, dynamic conception of architecture.

The direction of this research did not appear overnight. Around 1968, together with many in my generation of young architects, I was concerned with the need for an architecture that might change society—that could have a political or social effect. However, the effect of the events of 1968 has been to demonstrate, both through facts and through serious critical analysis, the difficulty of this imperative. From Marxist commentators to Henri Lefebvre and to the Situationists, the modes of analysis changed considerably, but all shared a skeptical view of the power of architecture to alter social or political structures.

Historical analysis has generally supported the view that the role of the architect is to project on the ground the images of social institutions, translating the economic or political structure of society into buildings or groups of buildings. Hence architecture was, first and foremost, the adaptation of space to the existing socioeconomic structure. It would serve the powers in place, and, even in the case of more socially oriented policies, its programs would reflect the prevalent views of the existing political framework. Such conclusions were, of course, unpleasant to arrive at for young architects who wanted to change the world through their designs. Many returned to life-as-usual and entered conventional practices. A minority, however, kept trying to understand the nature of the mechanisms that made our cities and their architecture, exploring whether there was not another angle to the story or another way to address the issue of architectural change.

Fascinated by the ability of the metropolis to generate unexpected social or cultural manifestations (and even micro-economic systems), I had started extensive research. How might it be possible to encourage such urban upheavals—"to design the conditions" rather than "to condition the design," as it was said at the time? The courses I was teaching at the Architectural Association in London in the early 1970s were entitled "Urban Politics" and "The Politics of Space." These lectures and seminars—distributed as leaflets printed on colored paper, to alleviate their serious tone—provided an important means by which to develop my argument.

One of these texts was entitled "The Environmental Trigger." It had been prepared for a symposium at the AA in 1972. I was twenty-eight then, and the extensive questioning it contained outlined my major concern: How could architecture and cities be a trigger for social and political change? I had been fascinated by the *détournement* of the Paris streets during the May events and began to perceive similar patterns of "misuse" in many large cities throughout the world. Due to the concentration of economic power in such urban centers, any actions, whether planned or spontaneous, would immediately take on unexpected dimensions. Not only was the city (Liverpool, London, Los Angeles,

Belfast, etc.) the place where social conflicts were most exacerbated but, I argued, the urban condition itself could be a means to accelerate social change. I went several times to Belfast and Derry using clandestine IRA contacts, gathering information with the aim of preparing an issue on urban insurgency for the magazine *Architectural Design*. (The project was finally aborted when publishers acted upon a rumor that bomb threats had disrupted a symposium on the subject at the AA.)

If "The Environmental Trigger" gave an overly optimistic account of the potential for economic collapse to generate social transformation, it also analyzed the potential role of the architect in the process of change. The question was: How could architects avoid seeing architecture and planning as the faithful product of dominant society, viewing their craft, on the contrary, as a catalyst for change? Could architects reverse the proposition and, instead of serving a conservative society that acted upon our cities, have the city itself act upon society? Twenty years later, my analysis has changed little and I will quote extensively from this early work. "Could space," I wrote,

> be made a peaceful instrument of social transformation, a means of changing the relationship between the individual and society by generating a new lifestyle? Minimal cells and community kitchens in revolutionary Russia were to be the social condensors that determined new relationships between people, acting as a mould of the society to come as well as its ideal reflection. If the failure of such attempts

in the rest of Europe (where no revolution had taken place) could be explained in terms of the absolute contradiction between a new spatial organization and ever-growing land speculation, their fate was not much different in countries in which the political situation had been more favorable to them.

A fundamental misunderstanding was the cause. Linked to the ideology of a pure and liberating technique, such theory was based on an interpretation of behaviorism, according to which individual behavior can be influenced, even rationalized, by the organization of space. If a spatial organization can temporarily modify individual or group behavior, this does not imply that it will change the socio-economic structure of a reactionary society.

The implication of this analysis was that an architectural space per se (space before its use) was politically neutral: an asymmetrical space, for example, was no more or no less revolutionary or progressive than a symmetrical one. (It was said at the time that there was no such thing as socialist or fascist architecture, only architecture in a socialist or fascist society.) Several precedents pointed, however, to the extraordinary power of incidents, of small actions amplified a thousand times by the media so as to assume the role of revolutionary myth. In these cases, it was not the form of architecture that counted (whether it was contextual or modernist), but the use (and meaning) that was assigned to it. I used the example of a mythical "guerilla" building constructed in three days in a derelict Paris suburb at the end of 1968 by students from the Ecole des Beaux-Arts, using materials "borrowed" from nearby construction sites:

> The guerilla building was architecturally just a shelter, a barrack on a building site, but it was called "The House of the People" and thus referred to meanings of freedom, equality, power, and so on. The space in itself was neutral, but in order to prove that it had a political meaning, specific signs to this effect were necessary so as to give it a name or, less crudely, to perform political acts involving building (in this case, erecting a building for the people on private or state property). It was a rhetorical act, and the only possible one, for the main reason for such acts was their symbolic and exemplary value in the seizure of the land, not in the design of what was built.

I then saw only three possible roles for architects. Either we could become conservative, that is, we would "conserve" our historical role as translators of, and form-givers to, the political and economic priorities of existing society. Or we could function as critics and commentators, acting as intellectuals who reveal the contradictions of society through writings or other forms of practice, sometimes outlining possible courses of actions, along with their strengths and limitations. Finally, we could act as revolutionaries by using our environmental knowledge (meaning our understanding of cities and the mechanisms of architecture) in order to be part of professional forces trying to arrive at new social and urban structures.

While I advocated a combination of the roles of critics and revolutionaries, I was also aware of the limitations of our position as intellectuals and architects who were unlikely to find ourselves loading guns and hiding explosives in underground networks. I therefore proposed two types of actions or strategies as possible political acts. I called these strategies "exemplary actions" and "counterdesign." The first was not specifically architectural but relied heavily on an understanding of urban structures. It also suggested the polarization of conflicts so as to destroy the most reactionary norms and values of our society.

"Exemplary actions" act as both the expression of and the catalyst for the environmental crisis, while they combine, in a guerilla tactic, useful immediacy with exemplarity, everyday life with awareness. For example, the three-day construction of a *"Maison du Peuple"* on seized land represents a most startling attempt to promote a guerilla architecture in the workers' suburbs of a large western European city. It can obviously be argued by the French students (in a typical Franz Fanon description of "action in order to become conscious of one's existence") that building an object collectively is a factor in unity and a good political school for the participants that allows links with the local population; that the existence of a free place, even if only temporary, is an important factor in the development of the revolutionary struggle; and that the self-defense of buildings endangered by police violence allows experimentation and reinforcement of the means of struggle.

But above all, the purposes of the exemplary action are demystification and propaganda; it means to reveal that the capitalist organization of space destroys all collective space in order to develop division and isolation, and that it is possible to build fast and cheaply with building methods that are in contradiction with the economic logic of the system. (It is implied that the underdevelopment of building methods is a direct result of private land property). The purpose is, therefore, not merely the realization of an object built for itself, but also the revelation through building of realities and contradictions of society.

The takeover of the closed Kentish Town Railroad Station in London with my AA students in November 1971, along with subsequent painting and squatting activities, went beyond the mere implementation of inflatable domes for community services. The five-minute attacks and the appropriation of space were the first steps to free urban use.

The second strategy was more architectural, insofar as it used the architect's means of expression (plans, perspectives, collages, etc.) in order to denounce the evil effects of planning practices imposed by conservative city boards and governments. Archizoom's *No-Stop City* and Superstudio's *Continuous Monument* (both ironic and critical projects from 1970) provided possible models for such an approach.

"Counterdesign" can be described as a desperate and nihilistic attempt to use one particular feature of architectural expression, with all its cultural values and connotations. It is desperate in that it relies on the weakest of all architectural means, the plan, since we have defined that, by nature, no built object could ever have an effect on the socioeconomic structure of a reactionary society. It is nihilistic in that its only role is to translate the pessimistic forecast of the intentions of the holders of financial power into an architectural statement.

This approach considers that the plan's weakness may only be apparent. As the plan is meant to be the end product, it acquires an additional freedom that no capital-bound built piece ever had. Its role is not to design a social alternative that would soon be mystified by the power groups that implement it, but simply to comprehend the official forces in an area, to predict their future and to translate them in graphical terms for explanation's sake. It is a graffiti business. Just as graffiti or a pornographic image bears an obscenity that the real thing ignores, the architectural drawing can support specific meanings that the everyday experience of the actual building prevents. It may be used not only to demonstrate the increasingly well-known absurdity of some redevelopment proposals, or to verify where the capitalist system is going, but also to confirm emerging doubts about the relevance of this particular mode of expression. It is thus a cultural statement as well as a political one.

It is political through the plan's embodiment of an analysis of the speculators' aims, along with propaganda, tactics of confusion, caricature, and demonstration by the absurd. By being the devil's advocate, counterdesign is aimed at creating an understanding in the people concerned by the implications of such developments on their everyday life, and at leading to their active rejection of such planning processes. It is cultural in that it attempts to cast doubt and impel reconsideration of the cultural values that are still attached to architecture. Since the graphic revealing of speculators' scandals is by no means going to lead to a restructuring of society, the long-term objective of tactics of the absurd is the destruction of some of its cultural values.

For artists from the revolutionary twenties to the radical Italian architectural scene of the early seventies—Archizoom and others—the destruction of the established culture and the development of a revolutionary art form have traditionally been considered prerequisites to social and economic change. If it is doubtful that the development of a new formal language ever had an effect on the structure of society, it is clear that the destruction of the old language had. Education and "the advice of experts" are means of maintaining the traditional structures in place, and their questioning is a necessary step towards any new approach.

While not denying the validity of this strategy, I then proceeded to show its limitations by pointing to the ease with which cultural institutions took rebellious and destructive attitudes and translated them into sophisticated forms of mainstream culture. Duchamp's urinal, after all, is now a revered museum artifact; revolutionary slogans of 1968 Paris walls gave new life to the rhetoric of commercial advertising. I then suggested that, even if counterdesign was one of our few available courses of action, it was vulnerable to what the French call "recuperation." A subversive cultural practice did not automatically mean that its end product would be so. Someone's critical or ironic proof using absurdist gestures could always become someone else's sincere proposal. Indeed, this period saw designs of Superstudio-like ideal cities emerging from schools of architecture, this time as well-intended alternative lifestyles. Architecture (or the drawings that represent it) has always been an ambiguous mode of expression, as multiple interpretations can always be given to it.

Weary of the difficulties prompted by the strategies of "exemplary actions" and "counterdesign," I concluded by proposing a form of subversive analysis that would use environmental knowledge to accelerate radical change. It would reveal the absurdity of our current condition as well as precipitate the downfall of the most socially repressive aspects of our culture and cities. However, the examples I gave at the time showed an optimistic view of the outcome of social struggles. As I write today, the urban conflicts in Northern Ireland have certainly not led to "new social organizations through the illuminating effects of environmental actions." The text concluded, however, that these conflicts could be only a first step, intended to unsettle a situation that itself might contain the seeds of a better social and urban condition.

"None of these environmental tactics leads directly to a new social structure," I stated. No doubt. Architecture and its spaces do not change society, but through architecture and the understanding of its effect, we can accelerate processes of change under way. (Similarly, architecture can always slow down these processes of change by implementing passéist forms of building and of use.)

The political argumentation of the time was taking place in a context that saw radical questioning invade the cultural sphere as well. A key slogan of 1968 was "Imagination takes power." I felt at the time that while many social and political activists were articulate about the mechanisms of power, they often forgot the first term of the equation: imagination. Among those who understood the power of invention were the Situationists, who by 1972 already seemed distant history. Yet the most radical moments of twentieth-century art, literature, or film could not be absent from a complete questioning of society. From the Futurists to Dada and the Surrealists, a whole range of precedents fascinated us. Anatole Kopp had also just published his celebrated *City and Revolution* on the different movements that followed the 1917 uprisings.

I was starting to realize that the old revolutionary concept of "taking advantage of the internal contradictions of society" was applicable to architecture and, in turn, could one day influence society. The internal contradictions of architecture had been there all along; they were part of its very nature: architecture was about two mutually exclusive terms—space and its use or, in a more theoretical sense, the concept of space and the experience of space. The interplay between space and activities appeared to me as a possible route to bypass some of the obstacles that accompanied many anxieties about the social and political role of architecture.

Indeed, any political discussion by critics and historians about the making of architecture had generally focused on the formal or physical aspects of buildings and cities, rarely raising the question of the events that took place in them. Just as the *détournement*, or rebellious use, of the urban physical framework had led to various types of urban upheaval, could the use and misuse of the architectural space lead to a new architecture? Over the next decade I kept exploring the implications of what had first been intuitions: (a) that there is no cause-and-effect relationship between the concept of space and the experience of space, or between buildings and their uses, or space and the movement of bodies within it, and (b) that the meeting of these mutually exclusive terms could be intensely pleasurable or, indeed, so violent that it could dislocate the most conservative elements of society.

Just as inherent oppositions had been identified between the urban framework and social movements, comparable oppositions could be witnessed between architectural space and its many possible uses. By arguing that there is no architecture without event or program, I could insert both programmatic and spatial concerns within the architectural discourse as well as within its representation. The debates taking place in other disciplines—art, literary criticism, and film theory among them—were confirming those first intuitions. Allies could be found in those other fields who would help demonstrate what I perceived as blinding evidence: architecture was, by definition, by nature, *disjoined, dis-sociated.* From Foucault to Barthes, from the activities of Sollers and the Tel Quel group to the rediscovery of Bataille, Joyce, or Burroughs, from the film theories of Eisenstein and Vertov to the experiments of Welles and Godard, from conceptual art to Acconci's early performances, an enormous body of work was helping to substantiate the evidence of architecture's dissociations. Those who say that architecture is impure if it must borrow its arguments from other disciplines not only forget the inevitable interferences of culture, economy, and politics but also underestimate the ability of architecture to accelerate the workings of culture by contributing to its polemic. As practice and as theory, architecture must import and export.

I must add here that too often architects do not see the relationship between theory and cultural work. They want to see theory as a means to arrive at, or justify, architectural form or practice. It is striking to notice, for example, the respective interpretations of postmodernism in the separate fields of art and architecture, whereby postmodernism in architecture became associated with an identifiable style, while in art it meant a critical practice.

In my case, theoretical writing had for its aim not only to expand architectural concepts but also to negotiate the relationship between the cultural practice of architecture and the interrelated spheres of politics, literature, or the arts. In no way was I interested in translating or transposing literary or film motives into architecture. Quite the contrary. But I also needed these allies to support a key architectural argument. The research in other fields corroborated my view that the inherent disjunction of architecture was its strength and its subversive power; that the disjunction between space and event, together with their inevitable cohabitation, was characteristic of our contemporary condition. Architecture, then, could not only import certain notions from other disciplines but could also export its findings into the production of culture. In this sense, architecture could be considered as a form of knowledge comparable to mathematics or philosophy. It could explore and expand the limits of our knowledge. It could also be intensely social and political, as architecture could not be separated from its very use.

Simultaneously, I tried to develop these concepts through other means—the drawings of *The Manhattan Transcripts,* the multiple and discontinuous buildings of the Parc de la Villette in Paris, along with numerous urban schemes, up to the "Le Fresnoy" project (Studio National des Arts Contemporains) in Tourcoing in northern France. Whether texts, drawings, or buildings, each mode of working provided further means of exploration. This is indeed one of the great characteristics of architectural work: you can also think through it. As I had written in the introduction to *The Manhattan Transcripts:*

> In architecture, concepts can either precede or follow projects or buildings. In other words, a theoretical concept may be either *applied* to a project or *derived* from it. Quite often this distinction cannot be made so clearly, when, for example, a certain aspect of film theory may support an architectural intuition, and later, through the arduous development of a project, be transformed into an operative concept for architecture in general.

Architecture's inherent confrontation of space and use and the inevitable disjunction of the two terms means that architecture is constantly unstable, constantly on the verge of change. It is paradoxical that three thousand years of architectural ideology have tried to assert the very opposite: that architecture is about stability, solidity, foundation. I would claim that architecture was used "*à contre-emploi*", against and despite itself, as society tried to employ it as a means to stabilize, to institutionalize, to establish permanence. Of course, this prevailing ideology meant that architecture had to ignore the other terms of its equation (i.e., to be nothing but "the artful building of spaces," "*le jeu correct et magnifique des volumes sous la lumière*"), or to coincide with frozen rituals of occupancy—a court of justice, a hospital, a church, even the vernacular one-family house— in which the rituals of the institution were directly reflected in the architectural spaces that enclosed them. Foucault's discussion on architecture and power ultimately echoed Sullivan's "form follows function."

Of course, from the pyramids of Egypt to the monuments of Rome to today's shopping centers, "clients" have seen architecture as a means by which institutions could manifest and solidify their presence in society. In doing so, the disjunction between various terms of the architectural equation—space, program, movement—had been suppressed. Not to include the uncertainties of use, action, and movement in the definition of architecture meant that the architecture's ability to be a factor of social change was simply denied.

Similarly, the most significant so-called deconstructive architectural challenges against order, hierarchy, and stability in the last two decades have been praised or attacked by critics for what they called a "style" or the "pursuit of aesthetic experimentation." These critics were unwittingly at risk of ignoring, not to say suppressing, the underlying discussion about program and use in this work, and, by extension, about the larger social, political, and even economic implications of architecture. By downplaying the programmatic dimension, they were repeating what they had accused others of doing in staging the 1932 International Style exhibition at MoMA in New York.

The new questioning of that part of architecture called "program," or "function," or "use," or "events," is fundamental today. Not only is there no simple relation between the building of spaces and the programs within them, but in our contemporary society, programs are by definition unstable. Few can decide what a school or a library should be or how electronic it should be, and perhaps fewer can agree on what a park in the twenty-first century should consist of. Whether cultural or commercial, programs have long ceased to be determinate, since they change all the time—while the building is designed, during its construction, and, of course, after completion. (At the Parc de la Villette, one building was first designed as a gardening center, then reorganized as a restaurant by the time the concrete framework was completed, and finally used—successfully— as a children's painting and sculpture workshop.)

What has been true for very large buildings (the ever-changing use of warehouses or of the new generation of American "big footprint" skyscrapers) also applies to the smallest constructions. There is no longer a causal relationship between buildings and their content, their use, and, of course, their very improbable meaning. Space and its usage are two opposed notions that exclude one another, generating an endless array of uncertainties. Not unlike developments in modern scientific knowledge that dismantled the mechanistic and determinate vision of classical science, here we see disorder, collisions, and unpredictabilities entering the field of architecture. While there still may be local certainties of specific or autonomous systems, the relationship between them is inevitably one of disjunction.

Yet it is in this very state of uncertainty that the new developments in architecture reside. Today, the two areas of investigation most likely to provide fertile discoveries are located in an extension of our two disjoined terms: spaces (through new technology and structures, or—to use the title of a conference at Columbia University—through "glue and microchips") and events (through new programmatic, functional, or social relations, through the spectacle of everyday life). One argument for the interchangeability of the two terms can be found in the new media technology that at once defines and activates space, such as electronic façades that are both enclosure and spectacle.

The definition of architecture as simultaneously space and event brings us back to political concerns, or more precisely, to the question of space as related to social practice. If architecture is neither pure form nor solely determined by socioeconomic or functional constraints, the search for its definition must always expand to an urban dimension. The complex social, economic, and political mechanisms that govern the expansion and contraction of the contemporary city are not without effect on architecture and its societal use. Space always marks the territory, the milieu of social practice. Would we ever wish it to do so, our society could not get out of its space. Even though it produces space, society is always its prisoner. Because space is the common framework for all activities, it is often used politically in order to give an appearance of coherence through the concealment of its social contradictions.

This conjoined/dis-joined condition characterizes our cities, our architecture. The contemporary world is a dislocated space of constraints that may find few common denominators. Yet we should remember that there is no social or political change without the movements and programs that transgress supposedly stable institutionality, architectural or otherwise; that there is no architecture without everyday life, movement, and action; and that it is the most dynamic aspects of their disjunctions that suggest a new definition of architecture.

I Space | essays written in 1975 and 1976

Fireworks, Manifesto, 1974.

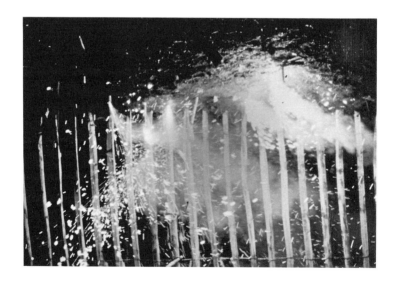

The Architectural Paradox

1. Most people concerned with architecture feel some sort of disillusion and dismay. None of the early utopian ideals of the twentieth century has materialized, none of its social aims has succeeded. Blurred by reality, the ideals have turned into redevelopment nightmares and the aims into bureaucratic policies. The split between social reality and utopian dream has been total, the gap between economic constraints and the illusion of all-solving technique absolute. Pointed out by critics who knew the limits of architectural remedies, this historical split has now been bypassed by attempts to reformulate the concepts of architecture. In the process, a new split appears. More complex, it is not the symptom of professional naiveté or economic ignorance but the sign of a fundamental question that lies in the very nature of architecture and of its essential element: space. By focusing on itself, architecture has entered an unavoidable paradox that is more present in space than anywhere else: the impossibility of questioning the nature of space and at the same time experiencing a spatial praxis.

2.   I have no intention of reviewing architectural trends and their connection to the arts. My general emphasis on space rather than on disciplines (art, architecture, semiology, etc.) is not aimed at negating academic categorization. The merging of disciplines is too worn a path to provide a stimulating itinerary. Instead, I would like to focus attention on the present paradox of space and on the nature of its terms, trying to indicate how one might go beyond this self-contradiction, even if the answer should prove intolerable. I begin by recalling the historical context of this paradox. I will examine first those trends that consider architecture as a thing of the mind, as a dematerialized or conceptual discipline, with its linguistic or morphological variations (the Pyramid); second, empirical research that concentrates on the senses, on the experience of space as well as on the relationship between space and praxis (the Labyrinth); and third, the contradictory nature of these two terms and the difference between the means of escaping the paradox by shifting the actual nature of the debate, as, for example, through politics, and the means that alter the paradox altogether (the Pyramid and the Labyrinth).

3. Etymologically, to define space means both "to make space distinct" and "to state the precise nature of space." Much of the current confusion about space can be illustrated by this ambiguity. While art and architecture have been concerned essentially with the first sense, philosophy, mathematics, and physics have tried throughout history to give interpretations to something variously described as a "material thing in which all material things are located" or as "something subjective with which the mind categorizes things." Remember: with Descartes ended the Aristotelian tradition according to which space and time were "categories" that enabled the classification of "sensory knowledge." Space became absolute. Object before the subject, it dominated senses and bodies by containing them. Was space inherent to the totality of what exists? This was the question of space for Spinoza and Leibniz. Returning to the old notion of category, Kant described space as neither matter nor the set of objective relations between things but as an ideal internal structure, an a priori consciousness, an instrument of knowledge. Subsequent mathematical developments on non-Euclidean spaces and their topologies did not eliminate the philosophical discussions. These reappeared with the widening gap between abstract spaces and society. But space was generally accepted as a *cosa mentale*, a sort of all-embracing set with subsets such as literary space, ideological space, and psychoanalytical space.

4. Architecturally, to define space (to make space distinct) literally meant "to determine boundaries." Space had rarely been discussed by architects before the beginning of the twentieth century. But by 1915 it meant *Raum* with all its overtones of German esthetics, with the notion of *Raum-empfindung* or "felt volume." By 1923 the idea of felt space had merged with the idea of composition to become a three-dimensional continuum, capable of metrical subdivision that could be related to academic rules. From then on, architectural space was consistently seen as a uniformly extended material to be modeled in various ways, and the history of architecture as the history of spatial concepts. From the Greek "power of interacting volumes" to the Roman "hollowed-out interior space," from the modern "interaction between inner and outer space" to the concept of "transparency," historians and theorists referred to space as a three-dimensional lump of matter.

To draw a parallel between the philosophies of a period and the spatial concepts of architecture is always tempting, but never was it done as obsessively as during the 1930s. Giedion related Einstein's theory of relativity to cubist painting, and cubist planes were translated into architecture in Le Corbusier's Villa Stein at Garches. Despite these space-time concepts, the notion of space remained that of a simplistic and amorphous matter to be defined by its physical boundaries. By the late 1960s, freed from the technological determinants of the postwar period and aware of recent linguistic studies, architects talked about the square, the street, and the arcade, wondering if these did not constitute a little-known code of space with its own syntax and meaning. Did language precede these socioeconomic urban spaces, did it accompany them, or did it follow them? Was space a condition or a formulation? To say that language preceded these spaces was certainly not obvious: human activities leave traces that may precede language. So was there a relationship between space and language, could one "read" a space? Was there a dialectic between social praxis and spatial forms?

5. Yet the gap remained between ideal space (the product of mental processes) and real space (the product of social praxis). Although such a distinction is certainly not ideologically neutral, we shall see that it is in the nature of architecture. As a result, the only successful attempts to bridge this philosophical gap were those that introduced historical or political concepts such as "production," in the wide sense it had in Marx's early texts. Much research in France and in Italy opposed space "as a pure form" to space "as a social product," space "as an intermediary" to space "as a means of reproduction of the mode of production."

This politico-philosophical critique had the advantage of giving an all-embracing approach to space, avoiding the previous dissociation between the "particular" (fragmented social space), the "general" (logico-mathematical or mental spaces), and the "singular" (physical and delineated spaces). But by giving an overall priority to historical processes, it often reduced space to one of the numerous socioeconomic products that were perpetuating a political status quo.[1]

6. Before proceeding to a detailed examination of the ambivalence of the definition of space, it is perhaps useful to consider briefly this particular expression of space in architecture. Its territory extends from an all-embracing "everything is architecture" to Hegel's minimal definition. This latter interpretation must be pointed out, for it describes a difficulty that is constitutive to architecture. When Hegel elaborated his aesthetic theory,[2] he conventionally distinguished five arts and gave them an order: architecture, sculpture, painting, music, and poetry. He started with architecture because he thought it preceded the others in both conceptual and historical terms. Hegel's uneasiness in these first pages is striking. His embarrassment did not really proceed from his conservative classification but was caused by a question that had haunted architects for centuries: were the functional and technical characteristics of a house or a temple the means to an end that excluded those very characteristics? Where did the shed end and architecture begin? Was architectural discourse a discourse about whatever did not relate to the "building" itself? Hegel concluded in the affirmative: architecture was whatever in a building did not point to utility. Architecture was a sort of "artistic supplement" added to the simple building. But the difficulty of such an argument appears when one tries to conceive of a building that escapes the utility of space, a building that would have no other purpose than "architecture."

Although such a question may be irrelevant, it finds a surprising echo in the present search for architectural autonomy. After more than half a century of scientific pretense, of system theories that defined it as the intersection of industrialization, sociology, politics, and ecology, architecture wonders if it can exist without having to find its meaning or its justification in some purposeful exterior need.

The Pyramid: Stating the Nature of Space (or The Dematerialization of Architecture)

7. Little concerned with Hegel's "artistic supplement," architects have nevertheless not regarded the constructed building as the sole and inevitable aim of their activity. They have shown a renewed interest in the idea of playing an active role in fulfilling ideological and philosophical functions with respect to architecture. Just as El Lissitzky and the Vesnin brothers sought to deny the importance of realizing a work and stressed an architectural attitude, so the avant-garde feels reasonably free to act within the realm of concepts. Comparable to the early conceptual artists' rejection of the art commodity market and its alienating effects, the architects' position seems justified by the very remote possibility they had of building anything other than a "mere reflection of the prevalent mode of production."

Moreover, historical precedents exist to give enough credibility to what could paradoxically be described either as a withdrawal from reality or as a takeover of new and unknown territories. "What is architecture?" asked Boullée. "Will I define it with Vitruvius as the art of building? No. This definition contains a crass error. Vitruvius takes the effect for the cause. One must conceive in order to make. Our forefathers only built their hut after they had conceived its image. This production of the mind, this creation is what constitutes architecture, that which we now can define as the art to produce any building and bring it to perfection. The art of building is thus only a secondary art that it seems appropriate to call the scientific part of architecture."[3] At a time when architectural memory rediscovers its role, architectural history, with its treatises and manifestos, has been conveniently confirming to architects that spatial concepts were made by the writings and drawings of space as much as by their built translations.

The questions, "is there any reason why one cannot proceed from design that can be constructed to design that concerns itself only with the ideology and concept of architecture?" and "if architectural work consists of questioning the nature of architecture, what prevents us from making this questioning a work of architecture in itself?"[4] were already rhetorical questions in 1972. The renewed importance given to conceptual aims in architecture quickly became established. The medium used for the communication of concepts became architecture; information was architecture; the attitude was architecture; the written program or brief was architecture; gossip was architecture; production was architecture; and inevitably, the architect was architecture. Escaping the predictable ideological compromises of building, the architect could finally achieve the sensual satisfaction that the making of material objects no longer provided.

8. The dematerialization of architecture into the realm of concepts was more the characteristic of a period than of any particular avant-garde group. Thus it developed in various directions and struck movements as ideologically opposed as, for example, "radical architecture"[5] and "rational architecture."[6] But the question it asked was fundamental: if everything was architecture, by virtue of the architect's decision, what distinguished architecture from any other human activity? This quest for identity revealed that the architect's freedom did not necessarily coincide with the freedom of architecture.

If architecture seemed to have gained freedom from the socioeconomic constraints of building processes, any radical counter-designs and manifestos were inevitably reinstated in the commercial circuits of galleries or magazines. Like conceptual art in the mid-1960s, architecture seemed to have gained autonomy by opposing the institutional framework. But in the process it had become the institutional opposition, thus growing into the very thing it tried to oppose.

Although some architects, following a political analysis that we shall soon describe, were in favor of doing away with architecture altogether, the search for autonomy inevitably turned back toward architecture itself, as no other context would readily provide for it. The question became: "Is there an architectural essence, a being that transcends all social, political, and economic systems?" This ontological bias injected new blood into a concept that already had been well aired by art theorists. Investigations into Hegel's "supplement" received the support of structural linguistic studies in France and Italy. Analogies with language appeared en masse, some useful, some particularly naive and misleading. Among these linguistic analogies, two figure prominently.

9. The first theory claims that the Hegelian "supplement," added to the simple building and constitutive of architecture, is immediately struck by some semantic expansion that would force this architectural supplement to be less a piece of architecture than the representation of something else. Architecture is then nothing but the space of representation. As soon as it is distinguished from the simple building, it represents something other than itself: the social structure, the power of the King, the idea of God, and so on.

The second theory questions an understanding of architecture as a language that refers to meanings outside itself. It refuses the interpretation of a three-dimensional translation of social values, for architecture would then be nothing but the linguistic product of social determinants. It thus claims that the architectural object is pure language and that architecture is an endless manipulation of the grammar and syntax of the architectural sign. Rational architecture, for example, becomes a selected vocabulary of architectural elements of the past, with their oppositions, contrasts, and redistributions. Not only does it refer to itself and to its own history, but function—the existential justification of the work—becomes virtual rather than real. So the language is closed in on itself, and architecture becomes a truly autonomous organism. Forms do not follow functions but refer to other forms, and functions relate to symbols. Ultimately architecture frees itself from reality altogether. Form does not need to call for external justifications. In a critical article in *Oppositions*, Manfredo Tafuri can thus describe Aldo Rossi's architecture as "a universe of carefully selected signs, within which the law of exclusion dominates, and in fact is the controlling expression," and the trend it represents as *"l'Architecture dans le Boudoir"* because the circle drawn around linguistic experimentation reveals a pregnant affinity with the obsessively rigorous writings of the Marquis de Sade.[7]

Freed from reality, independent of ideology, architectural values are striving toward a purity unattained since the Russian formalist criticism of the 1920s, when it was argued that the only valid object of literary criticism was the literary text. Here, the tautology of architecture—that is, an architecture that describes itself—becomes a syntax of empty signs, often derived from a selective historicism that concentrates on moments of history: the early modern movement, the Roman monument, the Renaissance palace, the castle. Transmitted through history, and removed from the constraints of their time, can these signs, these diagrams of spaces become the generative matrices of today's work?

10. They might. Architectural theory shares with art theory a peculiar characteristic: it is prescriptive. So the series of signs and articulations that has just been described may undoubtedly prove a useful model for architects engaged in a perpetual search for new support disciplines, even if it is not clear whether systems of nonverbal signs, such as space, proceed from concepts similar to verbal systems. However, the real importance of this research lies in the question it asks about the nature of architecture rather than in the making of architecture. This is not without recalling the perverse and hypothetical search for the very origins of architecture. Remember: at the outset, does architecture produce copies or models? If it cannot imitate an order, can it constitute one, whether it be the world or society? Must architecture create its own model, if it has no created model? Positive answers inevitably imply some archetype. But as this archetype cannot exist outside architecture, architecture must produce one itself. It thus becomes some sort of an essence that precedes existence. So the architect is once again "the person who conceives the form of the building without manipulating materials himself." He conceives the *pyramid*, this ultimate model of reason. Architecture becomes a *cosa mentale* and the forms conceived by the architect ensure the domination of the idea over matter.

The Labyrinth: Making Space Distinct (or The Experience of Space)

11. *Should I intensify the quarantine in the chambers of the Pyramid of reason? Shall I sink to depths where no one will*

*be able to reach me and understand me, living among ab-
stract connections more frequently expressed by inner mon-
ologues than by direct realities? Shall architecture, which
started with the building of tombs, return to the Tomb, to
the eternal silence of finally transcended history? Shall architecture perform at the service of illusory functions and
build virtual spaces? My voyage into the abstract realm of
language, into the dematerialized world of concepts, meant
the removal of architecture from its intricate and convo-
luted element: space. Removal from the exhilarating differences between the apse and the nave of Ely Cathedral,
between Salisbury Plain and Stonehenge, between the Street
and my Living Room. Space is real, for it seems to affect my
senses long before my reason. The materiality of my body
both coincides with and struggles with the materiality of
space. My body carries in itself spatial properties and spatial
determination: up, down, right, left, symmetry, dissymme-
try. It hears as much as it sees. Unfolding against the pro-
jections of reason, against the Absolute Truth, against the
Pyramid, here is the Sensory Space, the Labyrinth, the Hole.
Dislocated and dissociated by language or culture or economy into the specialized ghettos of sex and mind, Soho and
Bloomsbury, 42nd Street and West 40th Street, here is where
my body tries to rediscover its lost unity, its energies and
impulses, its rhythms and its flux . . .*

12. This purely sensory approach has been a recurrent theme
in this century's understanding and appreciation of space. It
is not necessary to expand at length on the precedents wit-

nessed by twentieth-century architecture. Suffice it to say that current conversation seems to fluctuate between (a) the German esthetic overtones of the *Raumempfindung* theory, whereby space is to be "felt" as something affecting the inner nature of man by a symbolic *Einfühlung,* and (b) an idea that echoes Schlemmer's work at the Bauhaus, whereby space was not only the medium of experience but also the materialization of theory. For example, the emphasis given to movement found in dance the "elemental means for the realization of space-creative impulses," for dance could articulate and order space. The parallel made between the dancer's movements and the more traditional means of defining and articulating space, such as walls or columns, is important. When the dancers Trisha Brown and Simone Forti reintroduced this spatial discussion in the mid-1960s, the relationship between theory and practice, reason and perception, had to take another turn, and the concept of theoretical praxis could not be simply indicative. There was no way in space to follow the art-language practice. If it could be argued that the discourse about art was art and thus could be exhibited as such, the theoretical discourse about space certainly was not space.

The attempt to trigger a new perception of space reopened a basic philosophical question. Remember: you are inside an enclosed space with equal height and width. Do your eyes instruct you about the cube merely by noticing it, without giving any additional interpretation? No. You don't really see the cube. You may see a corner, or a side, or the ceiling, but never all defining surfaces at the same time.

You touch a wall, you hear an echo. But how do you relate all these perceptions to one single object? Is it through an operation of reason?

13. This operation of reason, which precedes the perception of the cube as a cube, was mirrored by the approach of concept-performance artists. While your eyes were giving instructions about successive parts of the cube, allowing you to form the concept of cube, the artist was giving instructions about the concept of cube, stimulating your senses through the intermediary of reason. This reversal, this mirror image, was important, for the interplay between the new perception of "performance" space and the rational means at the origin of the piece was typically one aspect of the architectural process: the mechanics of perception of a distinct space, that is the complete space of the performance, with the movements, the thoughts, the received instructions of the actors, as well as the social and physical context in which they performed. But the most interesting part of such performance was the underlying discussion on the "nature of space" in general, as opposed to the shaping and perception of distinct spaces in particular.

It is in recent works that the recurring etymological distinction appears at its strongest. Reduced to the cold simplicity of six planes that define the boundaries of a more or less regular cube, the series of spaces designed by Bruce Nauman, Doug Wheeler, Robert Iwin, or Michael Asher do not play with elaborate spatial articulations. Their emphasis is elsewhere. By restricting visual and physical perception to the faintest of all stimulations, they turn the expected experience of the space into something altogether different. The almost totally removed sensory definition inevitably throws the viewers back on themselves. In "deprived space," to borrow the terminology of Germano Celant, the "participants" can only find themselves as the subject, aware only of their own fantasies and pulsations, able only to react to the low-density signals of their own bodies. The materiality of the body coincides with the materiality of the space. By a series of exclusions that become significant only in opposition to the remote exterior space and social context, the subjects only "experience their own experience."

14. Whether such spaces might be seen as reminiscent of the behaviorist spaces of the beginning of the century, where reactions were hopefully triggered, or as the new echo of the *Raumempfindung* theory, now cleaned-up of its moral and esthetic overtones, is of little theoretical importance. What matters is their double content: for their way to "make space distinct" (to define space in particular) is only there to throw one back on the interpretation of the "nature of space" itself. As opposed to the previously described pyramid of reason, the dark corners of experience are not unlike a *labyrinth* where all sensations, all feelings are enhanced, but where no overview is present to provide a clue about how to get out. Occasional consciousness is of little help, for perception in the Labyrinth presupposes immediacy. Unlike Hegel's classical distinction between the moment of perception and the moment of experience (when one's consciousness makes a new object out of a perceived one), the metaphorical Labyrinth implies that the first moment of perception carries the experience itself.

It is hardly surprising, therefore, that there may be no way out of the Labyrinth. Denis Hollier, in his book on Georges Bataille,[8] points out that from Bacon to Leibniz the Labyrinth was linked with the desire to get out, and science was seen as the means to find an exit. Rejecting such an interpretation, Bataille suggested that its only effect was to transform the Labyrinth into a banal prison. The traditional meaning of the metaphor was reversed: one never knows whether one is inside or not, since one cannot grasp it in one look. Just as language gives us words that encircle us but that we use in order to break their surround, the Labyrinth of experience was full of openings that did not tell whether they opened toward its outside or its inside.

The Pyramid and the Labyrinth: The Paradox of Architecture

15. To single out particular areas of concern, such as the rational play of language as opposed to the experience of the senses, would be a tedious game if it were to lead to a naive confrontation between the mind and the body. The architectural avant-garde has fought often enough over alternatives that appeared as opposites—structure and chaos, ornament and purity, permanence and change, reason and intuition. And often enough it has been shown that such alternatives were in fact complementary: our analysis of a dematerialization of architecture in its ontological form (the Pyramid) and of a sensual experience (the Labyrinth) is no different. But if the existence of such an equation does not raise doubts over its complementarity, it certainly raises questions about how such equations can go beyond the vicious circle of terms that speak only of themselves.

The answer may lie in the context in which such an equation takes place. A common accusation of analyses or even of works that concentrate on the specific nature of architecture is that they are "parallel," that is, they fold and unfold in some Panglossian world where social and economic forces are conveniently absent. Not affecting the determining forces of production, they constitute harmless forms of private expression. We shall therefore briefly consider the ambiguous particularities of the relationships between architecture and politics.

16. These have been well researched in the past few years. The role of architecture and planning has been analyzed in terms of a projection on the ground of the images of social institutions, as a faithful translation of the structures of society into buildings or cities. Such studies underline the difficulty architecture has in acting as a political instrument. Recalling the nostalgic and attenuated cry of the Russian revolutionary "social condensers" of the 1920s, some advocated the use of space as a peaceful tool of social transformation, as a means of changing the relation between the individual and society by generating new lifestyles. But the "clubs" and community buildings proposed not only required an existing revolutionary society but also a blind belief in an interpretation of behaviorism according to which individual behavior could be influenced by the organization of space. Aware that spatial organization may temporarily modify individual or group behavior, but does not imply that it will change the socioeconomic structure of a reactionary society, architectural revolutionaries looked for better grounds. Their attempts to find a socially relevant, if not revolutionary, role for architecture culminated in the years following the May 1968 events with "guerrilla" buildings, whose symbolic and exemplary value lay in their seizure of urban space and not in the design of what was built. On the cultural front, plans for a surrealistic destruction of established value systems were devised by Italian "radical" designers. This nihilistic prerequisite for social and economic change was a desperate attempt to use the architect's mode of expression to denounce institutional trends by translating them into architectural terms, ironically "verifying where the system was going" by designing the cities of a desperate future.

Not surprisingly, it was the question of the production system that finally led to more realistic proposals. Aimed at redistributing the capitalistic division of labor, these proposals sought a new understanding of the technicians' role in building, in terms of a responsible partnership directly involved in the production cycle, thus shifting the concept of architecture toward the general organization of building processes.

17. Yet it is the unreal (or unrealistic) position of the artist or architect that may be its very reality. Except for the last attitude, most political approaches suffered from the predictable isolation of schools of architecture that tried to offer their environmental knowledge to the revolution. Hegel's architecture, the "supplement," did not seem to have the right revolutionary edge. Or did it? Does architecture, in its long-established isolation, contain more revolutionary power than its numerous transfers into the objective realities of the building industry and social housing? Does the social function of architecture lie in its very lack of function? In fact, architecture may have little other ground.

Just as the surrealists could not find the right compromise between scandal and social acceptance, architecture seems to have little choice between autonomy and commitment, between the radical anachronism of Schiller's "courage to talk of roses" and society. If the architectural piece renounces its autonomy by recognizing its latent ideological and financial dependency, it accepts the mechanisms of society. If it sanctuarizes itself in an art-for-art's-sake position, it does not escape classification among existing ideological compartments.

So architecture seems to survive only when it saves its nature by negating the form that society expects of it. *I would therefore suggest that there has never been any reason to doubt the necessity of architecture, for the necessity of architecture is its non-necessity. It is useless, but radically so.* Its radicalism constitutes its very strength in a society where profit is prevalent. Rather than an obscure artistic supplement or a cultural justification for financial manipulations, architecture is not unlike fireworks, for these "empirical apparitions," as Adorno puts it, "produce a delight that cannot be sold or bought, that has no exchange value and cannot be integrated in the production cycle."[9]

18. It is hardly surprising, therefore, that the non-necessity of architecture, its necessary loneliness, throws it back on itself. If its role is not defined by society, architecture will have to define it alone. Until 1750, architectural space could rely on the paradigm of the ancient precedent. After that time, until well into the twentieth century, this classical source of unity progressively became the socially determined program. In view of the present-day polarization of ontological discourse and sensual experience, I am well aware that any suggestion that they now form the inseparable but mutually exclusive terms of architecture requires some elucidation. This must begin with a description of the apparent impossibility of escaping from the paradox of the Pyramid of concepts and the Labyrinth of experience, of immaterial architecture as a concept and of material architecture as a presence.

To restate my point, the paradox is not about the impossibility of perceiving both architectural concept (the six faces of the cube) and real space at the same time but about the impossibility of questioning the nature of space and at the same time making or experiencing a real space. Unless we search for an escape from architecture into the general organization of building processes, the paradox persists: architecture is made of two terms that are interdependent but mutually exclusive. Indeed, *architecture constitutes the reality of experience while this reality gets in the way of the overall vision. Architecture constitutes the abstraction of absolute truth, while this very truth gets in the way of feeling.* We cannot both experience and think that we experience. "The concept of dog does not bark";[10] the concept of space is not in space.

In the same way, the achievement of architectural reality (building) defeats architectural theory while at the same time being a product of it. So theory and praxis may be dialectic to one another, but in space, the translation of the concept, the overcoming of the abstraction in reality, involves the dissolution of the dialectic and an incomplete statement. This means, in effect, that, perhaps for the first time in history, architecture can never be. The effect of the great battles of social progress is obliterated, and so is the security of archetypes. Defined by its questioning, architecture is always the expression of a lack, a shortcoming, a noncompletion. It always misses something, either reality or concept. Architecture is both being and nonbeing. The only alternative to the paradox is silence, a final nihilistic statement that might provide modern architectural history with its ultimate punchline, its self-annihilation.

19. Before leaving this brief exploration of architecture as paradox, it is tempting to suggest a way of accepting the paradox while refuting the silence it seems to imply. This conclusion may be intolerable to philosophers, in that it alters the subject of architecture, you and I. It may be intolerable to scientists who want to master the subject of science. It may be intolerable to artists who want to objectify the subject.

Let us first examine the Labyrinth. In the course of this argument, it has been implied that the Labyrinth shows itself as a slow history of space, but that a total revelation of the Labyrinth is historically impossible because no point of transcendence in time is available. One can participate in and share the fundamentals of the Labyrinth, but one's perception is only part of the Labyrinth as it manifests itself. One can never see it in totality, nor can one express it. One is condemned to it and cannot go outside and see the whole. But remember: Icarus flew away, toward the sun. So after all, does the way out of the Labyrinth lie in the making of the Pyramid, through a projection of the subject toward some transcendental objectivity? Unfortunately not. The Labyrinth cannot be dominated. The top of the Pyramid is an imaginary place, and Icarus fell down: the nature of the Labyrinth is such that it entertains dreams that include the dream of the Pyramid.

20. But the real importance of the Labyrinth and of its spatial experience lies elsewhere. The Pyramid, the analysis of the architectural object, the breaking down of its forms and elements, all cut away from the question of the subject. Along with the spatial praxis mentioned earlier, the sensual architecture reality is not experienced as an abstract object already transformed by consciousness but as an immediate and concrete human activity—as a praxis, with all its subjectivity. This importance of the subject is in clear opposition to all philosophical and historical attempts to objectify the immediate perception of reality, for example, in the relations of production. To talk about the Labyrinth and its praxis means to insist here on its subjective aspects: it is personal and requires an immediate experience. Opposed to Hegel's *Erfahrung* and close to Bataille's "interior experience," this immediacy bridges sensory pleasure and reason. It introduces new articulations between the inside and the outside, between private and public spaces. It suggests new oppositions between dissociated terms and new relations between homogeneous spaces. This immediacy does not give precedence to the experiential term, however. *For it is only by recognizing the architectural rule that the subject of space will reach the depth of experience and its sensuality. Like eroticism, architecture needs both system and excess.*

21. This "experience" may have repercussions that go far beyond man as its "subject." Torn between rationality and the demand for irrationality, our present society moves toward other attitudes. If system plus excess is one of its symptoms, we may soon have to consider architecture as the indispensable complement to this changing praxis. In the past, architecture gave linguistic metaphors (the Castle, the Structure, the Labyrinth) to society. It may now provide the cultural model.

As long as social practice rejects the paradox of ideal and real space, imagination—interior experience—

may be the only means to transcend it. By changing the prevalent attitudes toward space and its subject, the dream of the step beyond the paradox can even provide the conditions for renewed social attitudes. Just as eroticism is the pleasure of excess rather than the excess of pleasure, so the solution of the paradox is the imaginary blending of the architecture rule and the experience of pleasure.

E. A. Dupont, *Variety,* 1925.

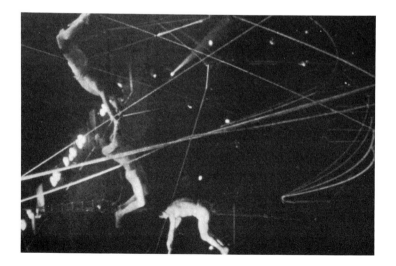

Questions of Space

1 . 0 Is space a material thing in which all material things are to be located?

1 . 1 If space is a material thing, does it have boundaries?

1 . 1 1 If space has boundaries, is there another space outside those boundaries?

1 . 1 2   If space does not have boundaries, do things then extend infinitely?

1 . 1 2 1   As every finite extent of space is infinitely divisible (since every space can contain smaller spaces), can an infinite collection of spaces then form a finite space?

1 . 1 3   In any case, if space is an extension of matter, can one part of space be distinguished from another?

1 . 2   If space is not matter, is it merely the sum of all spatial relations between material things?

1 . 3   If space is neither matter nor a set of objective relations between things, is it something subjective with which the mind categorizes things?

1 . 3 1   If the structure of the mind imposes an a priori form (that precedes all experience) to the perception of the external world, is space such a form?

1 . 3 2   If space is such a form, does it have precedence over all other perceptions?

1 . 4   If, etymologically, "defining" space is both making space distinct and stating the precise nature of space, is this an essential paradox of space?

1 . 5   Architecturally, if defining space is making space distinct, does making space distinct define space?

1 . 5 1   If architecture is the art of making space distinct, is it also the art of stating the precise nature of space?

1 . 6   Is architecture the concept of space, the space, and the definition of space?

1 . 6 1   If the concept of space is not a space, is the materialization of the concept of space a space?

1 . 6 1 1   Is conceptual space then the space of which material is the concept?

1 . 6 1 2   Incidentally, is the experience of the materialization of the concept of space the experience of space?

1 . 6 2   If the materialization of the concept of space is a space, then is space a hole in a space that it is not?

1 . 6 3   If the history of architecture is the history of spatial concepts, is space as a uniformly extensive material to be modeled in various ways at the origin of architectural space as (a) the power of volumes and their interaction; (b) hollowed-out interior space; (c) the interaction between inner and outer space; (d) the presence of absence?

1 . 6 3 1   Does a De Stijl facade differ from a baroque one through the microspace it defines?

1 . 7   If Euclidean space is restricted to a three-dimensional lump of matter, is non-Euclidean space to be restricted to a series of events in four-dimensional space-time?

1 . 7 1   If other geometries give a clearer understanding of space than Euclidean geometry, has space itself changed with the construction of spaces with d-dimensions?

1 . 7 2   Is topology a mental construction toward a theory of space?

2 . 0   Is the perception of space common to everyone?

2 . 1   If perceptions differ, do they constitute different worlds that are the products of one's past experience?

2 . 2   If space consciousness is based on one's respective experience, then does the perception of space involve a gradual construction rather than a ready-made schema?

2 . 2 1   Does this gradual construction contain elements that have a degree of invariance, such as archetypes?

2 . 3   Are spatial archetypes inevitably of a universal elementary nature, or can they include personal idiosyncracies?

2 . 4   If space is a basic a priori category of consciousness, independent of matter, is it an instrument of knowledge?

2 . 5   Is an instrument of knowledge the medium of experience?

2 . 5 1   Since it can be said that experience is contained within the nature of practice, is space inextricably bound up with practice?

2 . 5 2   Architecturally, if space is the medium for the materialization of theory, is a space the materialization of the architectural concept?

2 . 6   Is the materialization of architecture necessarily material?

2 . 6 1   Is the dematerialization of architecture necessarily immaterial?

2 . 7   Is the experience of space the experience of the materialization of the concept of space? Or of any concept?

2 . 7 1   Can a geometrical spatial concept be replaced by a concept based on one's experience of space?

2 . 7 2   Does the experience of space determine the space of experience?

2 . 7 3   If such a question is said to be absurd, does (architectural) space exist independently of the experiencing body?

2 . 8   If space is neither an external object nor an internal experience (made of impressions, sensations and feelings), are space and ourselves inseparable?

2 . 8 1   Are objective social space and subjective inner space then inextricably bound together?

2 . 9   Is space thus one of the structures that expresses our "being" in the world?

3 . 0   Is there a language of space (a space-language)?

3 . 1   Do all spaces in society taken together constitute a language?

3 . 1 1   Is a selection from this totality a set of spaces (which, of course, can be called a space of spaces)?

3 . 1 2   If space (singular, indefinite) is collective and permanent, are spaces (plural, definite) individual and transformable?

3 . 2   If a definite space is a thing that can be referred to, can it become a symbol (a form that will signify)?

3 . 2 1   If a definite space can become a sign or symbol, can it signify a thought or a concept?

3 . 3   (For linguists only.) If space is just a thing, (a) does it determine thought and language; (b) together with thought, is it determined by language; (c) together with language, is it determined by thought?

3 . 3 1   (For you and me.) Does a↔b↔c↔a?

3 . 4   If a space is a representation of an idea or a thought that is signified, does a space achieve its meaning through its relation to all the other spaces in a context, or through all the spaces for which this space has become metaphorical?

3 . 4 1   If there are different modes and uses of language, can space thus be classified into scientific, mythical, technological, logico-mathematical, fictive, poetic, rhetorical, critical spaces?

3 . 4 2   Does the explicit classification of the various meanings, modes, and uses of space destroy the experience of that space?

3 . 4 2 1   Can a space (stylistic form) be separated from the space that is a dimension of the meaning embodied in its architecture?

3 . 5   In any case, does the concept of space note and denote all possible spaces, both real and virtual?

3 . 5 1   If the understanding of all possible spaces includes social and mental space as well as physical space without any distinction, is the distinction between living, perceiving, and conceiving space a necessary condition of that understanding?

4 . 0   Is space the product of historical time?

4 . 1   Does the Hegelian end of history mean the end of space as a product of history?

4 . 2   On the other hand, if history does not end, and historical time is the Marxist time of revolution, does space lose its primary role?

4 . 3   If space is neither a social product (an end result) nor a pure category (a starting point), is it an in-between (an intermediary)?

4 . 4   If space is an in-between, is it a political instrument in the hands of the state, a mould
as well as a reflection of society?

4 . 5   If space is a three-dimensional mold that reflects the means of production, does it ensure
the survival of the state?

4 . 6   If three-dimensional space does not ensure
the survival of the state, is space the means
of reproduction of the mode of production?

4 . 6 1   If space is not simply the place where objects
are produced and exchanged, has it become
the very object of production?

4 . 6 2   If the truth of political economy can pervade
the truth of revolution, can the concept of
production pervade the concept of space?

4 . 7   Does the truth of revolution lie in the permanent expression of subjectivity?

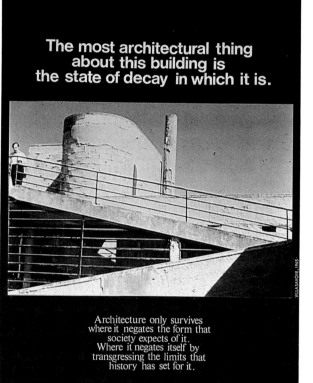

Architecture and Transgression

Transgression opens the door into what lies beyond the limits usually observed, but it maintains these limits just the same. Transgression is complementary to the profane world, exceeding its limits but not destroying it.

Georges Bataille, *Eroticism*

One issue rarely raised in architecture is that of taboo and transgression. Although society secretly delights in crime, excesses, and violated prohibitions of all sorts, there seems to be a certain puritanism among architectural theorists. They easily argue about rules but rarely debate their transgression. From Vitruvius to Quatremère de Quincy, from Durand to modern movement writers, architectural theory is primarily the elaboration of rules, whether based on an analysis of historical tradition or on a New Man (as the twenties' architects conceived it). From the *système des Beaux-Arts* to computer-aided design, from functionalism to typologies, from the accepted rules to the invented ones, there is a comprehensive and ever-present network of protective precepts. However, my purpose here is not to criticize the notion of rules nor to propose new ones. On the contrary, this essay will attempt to demonstrate that transgression is a whole, of which architectural rules are merely one part.

Before speaking about transgression, however, it is first necessary to recall the paradoxical relationship between architecture as a product of the mind, as a conceptual and dematerialized discipline, and architecture as the sensual experience of space and as a spatial praxis.

Part One: The Paradox

If one has a passion for the absolute that cannot be healed, there is

no other way out than to constantly contradict oneself and to rec-

oncile opposite extremes.

Frederic Schlegel

The very fact that something is written here makes it part of the field of architectural representation. Whether I use words, plans, or pictures, each page of this publication could be likened to the mythological world of Death: that is, it benefits from the privilege of extraterritoriality; it is outside architecture; it is outside the reality of space. Words and plans are safeguarded among mental constructs. They are removed from real life, subjectivity, and sensuality. Even when the words of the printed page are metamorphosed into slogans sprayed on city walls, they are nothing but a discourse. Boullée's aphorism that "the production of the mind is what constitutes architecture" merely underlines the importance of conceptual aims in architecture, but it excludes the sensual reality of spatial experience altogether.

A debate at a conceptual architecture conference in London[1] (where the majority of contributors predictably concluded that "all architecture is conceptual") emphasized the strange paradox that seems to haunt architecture: namely, the impossibility of simultaneously questioning the nature of space and, at the same time, making or experiencing a real space. The controversy indirectly reflected the prevalent architectural attitudes of the past decade. If the political implications of the production of building had been abundantly emphasized in the years following the 1968 crisis, the subsequent Hegelian reaction was revealing: "architecture is whatever in a building does not point to utility,"[2] and of course, by extension, whatever cannot be the mere three-dimensional projection of ruling socioeconomic structures, as theorists of urban politics were then maintaining. This emphasis on what Hegel called the "artistic supplement added to the simple building"—that is, on the immaterial quality that made it "architectural"—was no return to the old dichotomy between technology and cultural values. On the contrary, it set an ambiguous precedent for those "radical" architects who did not regard the constructed building as the sole and inevitable aim of their activity. Initially intended as an ideological means of stressing architectural "avant-garde attitudes" and refusing capitalist constraints, the work of such "radical" Italian or Austrian groups of the late 1960s was an attempt to dematerialize architecture into the realm of concepts.[3] The subsequent statement, "everything is architecture," had more affinities with conceptual art than with all-inclusive eclecticism. But if everything was architecture, how could architecture distinguish itself from any other human activity or from any other natural phenomenon?

Structural linguistic studies developed in the 1960s in France and Italy conveniently suggested a possible answer: analogies with language appeared everywhere, some useful, some particularly misleading. The chief characteristic of these analogies was their insistence on concepts. Whether these theorists stated that architecture always represented something other than itself—the idea of God, the power of institutions, and so on—or whether they took issue with the interpretation of architecture as a (linguistic) product of social determinants (and thus insisted on the autonomy of an architecture that only referred to itself, to its own language and history), their discourse reintroduced *rules* that were to govern architectural work by making use of old concepts such as types and models.[4]

This constant questioning about the nature of architecture only underlined the inevitable split between discourse and the domain of daily experience.[5] The architectural paradox had intruded once more. By definition architectural concepts were absent from the experience of space. Again, *it was impossible to question the nature of space* and at the same time make or experience a real space. The complex opposition between ideal and real space was certainly not ideologically neutral, and the paradox it implied was fundamental.

Caught, then, between sensuality and a search for rigor, between a perverse taste for seduction and a quest for the absolute, architecture seemed to be defined by the questions it raised. *Was architecture really made of two terms that were interdependent but mutually exclusive?* Did architecture constitute the reality of subjective experience while this reality got in the way of the overall concept? Or did architecture constitute the abstract language of absolute truth while this very language got in the way of feeling? Was architecture thus always the expression of a lack, of a shortcoming, or something incomplete? And if so, did architecture always necessarily miss either the reality or the concept? Was the only alternative to the paradox silence, a final nihilistic statement that would provide modern architectural history with its ultimate punchline, its self-annihilation?

Such questions are not rhetorical. It may be tempting to answer yes to all of them and accept the paralyzing consequences of a paradox that recalls philosophical battles of the past—Descartes versus Hume, Spinoza versus Nietzsche, Rationalists versus *Raumempfindung* symbolists.[6] It is even more tempting, however, to suggest another way around this paradox, to refute the silence the paradox seems to imply, even if this alternative proves intolerable.

Part Two: eROTicism

It appears that there is a certain point in the mind wherefrom life and death, reality and imaginary, past and future, the communicable and the incommunicable cease to be perceived in a contradictory way.

André Breton, *The Second Manifesto*

Paradoxes equivocate. They lie, and they don't; they tell the truth, and they don't. Each meaning has always to be taken with the others. The experience of the liar paradox is like standing between two mirrors, its meanings infinitely reflected. The paradox is literally speculative. To explore it, it is useful to consider two correspondences[7] without which much remains obscure.[8]

First Correspondence　The first correspondence is obvious and immediate. It is the correspondence of eroticism. Not to be confused with sensuality, eroticism does not simply mean the pleasure of the senses. Sensuality is as different from eroticism as a simple spatial perception is different from architecture. "Eroticism is not the excess of pleasure, but the pleasure of excess": this popular definition mirrors our argument. Just as the sensual experience of space does not make architecture, the pure pleasure of the senses does not constitute eroticism. On the contrary, "the pleasure of excess" requires consciousness as well as voluptuousness. Just as eroticism means a double pleasure that involves both mental constructs and sensuality, the resolution of the architectural paradox calls for architectural concepts and, at the same instant, the immediate experience of space. Architecture has the same status, the same function, and the same meaning as eroticism. At the possible/impossible junction of concepts and experience, architecture appears as the image of two worlds: personal and universal. Eroticism is no different; for one whose concept leads to pleasure (excess), eroticism is personal by nature. And by nature it is also universal. Thus, on the one hand, there is sensual pleasure, the other and the I; on the other hand, there is historical inquiry and ultimate rationality. Architecture is the ultimate erotic object, because an architectural act, brought to the level of excess, is the only way to reveal both the traces of history and its own immediate experiential truth.[9]

Second Correspondence   The junction between ideal space and real space is seen differently in the second correspondence. This second correspondence is immensely general and inevitably contains the present argument as it would contain many others. It is nothing less than the analogy of life-and-death, applied here to one celebrated architectural example.

Each society expects architecture to reflect its ideals and domesticate its deeper fears. And architecture and its theorists rarely negate the form that the society expects of it. Loos's celebrated attack on the intrinsic criminality of ornament was echoed by the modern movement's admiration for engineering "purity," and its admiration was translated into architectural terms by an unconscious consensus. "The engineers fabricate the tools of their time—everything except moth-eaten boudoirs and moldy houses. . . ."[10] This consistent repudiation of the so-called obscene scrawl[11] (as opposed to the puritan sense of hygiene) is not unlike mankind's horror for decaying and putrefied bodies. Death is tolerated only when the bones are white: if architects cannot succeed in their quest for "healthy and virile, active and useful, ethical and happy"[12] people and houses, they can at least be comfortable in front of the white ruins of the Parthenon. Young life and decent death, such was the architectural order.

Calling itself modern as well as independent of the bourgeois rules of the time, the heroic tradition of the 1930s nevertheless reflected the deep and unconscious fears of society. Life was seen as a negation of death—it condemned death and even excluded it—a negation that went beyond the idea of death itself and extended to the rot of the putrefying flesh. The anguish about death, however, only related to the phase of decomposition, for white bones did not possess the intolerable aspect of corrupted flesh. Architecture reflected these deep feelings: putrefying buildings were seen as unacceptable, but dry white ruins afforded decency and respectability. From being respectful to seeking respectability, there is only one step. Were the rationalists or the "New York Five" unconsciously striving for respect through the white and timeless skeletons they proposed?

Moreover, the fear of decaying organisms— as opposed to the nostalgic search for the "outmoded purity of architecture"—appears in conservationist enterprises as much as in utopian projects. Those who in 1965 visited the then derelict Villa Savoye certainly remember the squalid walls of the small service rooms on the ground floor, stinking of urine, smeared with excrement, and covered with obscene graffiti. Not surprisingly, the long campaign to save the threatened purity of the Villa Savoye doubled in intensity in the months that followed, and finally succeeded.

Society scares easily at those aspects of sensuality that it qualifies as obscene. "*Inter faeces et urinam nascimus*" (we are born between excrement and urine), wrote St. Augustine. In fact, the connection between death, fecal matter, and menstrual blood has often been demonstrated. In his studies of eroticism, Georges Bataille,[13] Le Corbusier's contemporary, pointed out that the fundamental prohibitions of mankind were centered on two radically opposed domains: death and its obverse, sexual reproduction. As a result, any discourse about life, death, and putrification implicitly contained a discourse on sex. Bataille claimed that at the key moment when life moved toward death, there could no longer be reproduction but only sex. Since eroticism implied sex without reproduction, the movement from life to death was erotic; "eroticism is assenting to life up to the point of death," wrote Bataille.

Just as Bataille's approach was certainly not exempt from the social taboos of his time, similar taboos surrounded many of the modern movement's attitudes. The modern movement loved both life and death, but separately. Architects generally do not love that part of life that resembles death: decaying constructions—the dissolving traces that time leaves on buildings—are incompatible with both the ideology of modernity and with what might be called conceptual esthetics. But in the opinion of this author— which is admittedly subjective—the Villa Savoye was never so moving as when plaster fell off its concrete blocks. While the puritanism of the modern movement and its followers has often been pointed out, its refusal to recognize the passing of time has rarely been noticed. (Not surprisingly, glass and glazed tiles have been among the preferred materials of the movement—for they do not reveal the traces of time.)

But to pursue this distasteful demonstration to the logical point where the distinction between argument and metaphor becomes blurred, it is my contention that the *moment of architecture* is that moment when architecture is life and death at the same time, when the experience of space becomes its own concept. In the paradox of architecture, the contradiction between architectural concept and sensual experience of space resolves itself at one point of

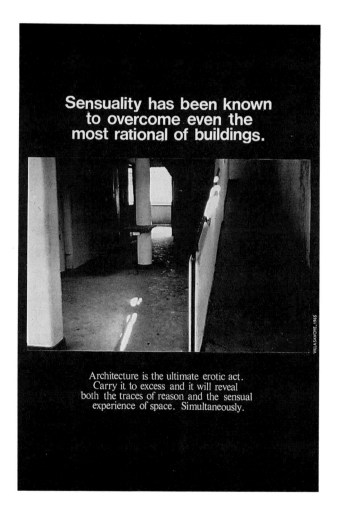

tangency: *the rotten point,* the very point that taboos and culture have always rejected. This metaphorical rot is where architecture lies. Rot bridges sensory pleasure and reason.

Part Three: The Transgression

Living in conformity with the archetypes amounted to respecting the 'law' . . . through the repetition of paradigmatic gestures, archaic man succeeded in annulling time.

Mircea Eliade, *Cosmos and History*

I was subject to respecting too much in my youth.

Stendhal, *Souvenirs d'égotisme*

It is tempting to leave the argument here and let the reader determine where this metaphorical rot becomes architecture and where architecture becomes erotic. For like eroticism, the phenomenon described here is of universal nature, although the suggested attitudes are subjective and particular. However, it is important to underline exactly what the two correspondences imply.

First, the two correspondences—that of rot and that of life and death—are aspects of the same phenomenon. In both cases, the meeting point of ideal and real space is a proscribed place; just as it is forbidden to experience pleasure while thinking about it, it is forbidden to look at the place where life touches death: Orpheus is not allowed to watch Eurydices' passage from death to life.

The life-and-death correspondence material-
izes the meeting place: the meeting place becomes the memory of life between death, the rotten place where spatial
praxis meets mental constructs, the convergence of two interdependent but mutually exclusive aspects.

Second, and very literally, such a place may
possess the moldy traces that time leaves on built form, the
soiled remnants of everyday life, the inscriptions of man or
of the elements—all, in fact, that *marks* a building.

Third, by extension, this meeting place is a
threat to the autonomy of, and the distinction between, concepts and spatial praxis. We have seen the beaux-arts architects at the turn of the century display blindness toward pure
engineering structures, and most contemporary architects
close their eyes to the traces of decay. Of course, the taboos
that haunt architects are hardly surprising. To paraphrase
Thomas Kuhn in *The Structure of Scientific Revolutions,*
most architects work from paradigms acquired through education and through subsequent exposure to architectural
literature, often without knowing what characteristics have
given these paradigms the status of rules or, by inversion,
that such paradigms imply subsequent taboos. These para-
digms-taboos may be more binding and more complex than
any set of rules that might be abstracted from them; they
remain entrenched because of the difficulty in unveiling the
hidden rules that have guided the particular architectural
approaches that generated them. Rules stay obscured, for
schools of architecture never teach concepts or theories in
the abstract. As a result, architects' perceptions are often as

culturally conditioned as those of a school child, even if the nature of this conditioning changes throughout history.

Fourth, by a further extension, the meeting place is ultimately architecture. It thrives on its ambiguous location between cultural autonomy and commitment, between contemplation and habit. Architecture seems to survive in its erotic capacity only wherever it *negates* itself, where it transcends its paradoxical nature by negating the form that society expects of it. In other words, it is not a matter of destruction or avant-garde subversion but of *transgression.*

While recently the rules called for the rejection of ornament, today's sensibility has changed, and purity is under attack. In a similar way, while the crowded street of the turn of the century was criticized by CIAM's theories of urban fragmentation, today the ruling status of the social and conceptual mechanisms eroding urban life is already the next to be transgressed.

Whether through literal or phenomenal transgression, architecture is seen here as the momentary and sacrilegious convergence of real space and ideal space. Limits remain, for transgression does not mean the methodical destruction of any code or rule that concerns space or architecture. On the contrary, it introduces new articulations between inside and outside, between concept and experience. Very simply it means overcoming unacceptable prevalences.

El Lissitzky, *Tatlin at Work,* **1922.**

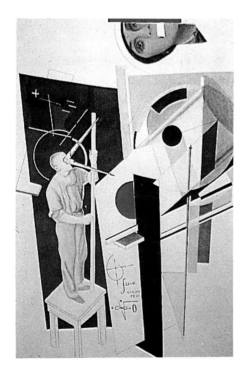

The Pleasure of Architecture

———

Functionalist dogmas and the puritan attitudes of the modern movement have often come under attack. Yet the ancient idea of pleasure still seems sacrilegious to contemporary architectural theory. For many generations any architect who aimed for or attempted to experience pleasure in architecture was considered decadent. Politically, the socially conscious have been suspicious of the slightest trace of hedonism in architectural endeavors and have rejected it as a reactionary concern. And in the same way, architectural conservatives have relegated to the Left everything remotely intellectual or political, including the discourse of pleasure. On both sides, the idea that architecture can possibly exist without either moral or functional justification, or even responsibility, has been considered distasteful.

Similar oppositions are reflected throughout the recent history of architecture. The avant-garde has endlessly debated oppositions that are mostly complementary: order and disorder, structure and chaos, ornament and purity, rationality and sensuality. And these simple dialectics have pervaded architectural theory to such an extent that architectural criticism has reflected similar attitudes: the purists' ordering of form versus art nouveau's organic sensuousness; Behrens's ethic of form versus Olbrich's impulse to the formless.

Often these oppositions have been loaded with moral overtones. Adolf Loos's attack on the criminality of ornament masked his fear of chaos and sensual disorder. And De Stijl's insistence on elementary form was not only a return to some anachronistic purity but also a deliberate regression to a secure order.

So strong were these moral overtones that they even survived Dada's destructive attitudes and the surrealists' abandonment to the unconscious. Tzara's ironical contempt for order found few equivalents among architects too busy replacing the *système des Beaux-Arts* by the modern movement's own set of rules. In 1920—despite the contradictory presences of Tzara, Richter, Ball, Duchamp, and Breton—Le Corbusier and his contemporaries chose the quiet and acceptable route of purism. Even in the early 1970s, the work of the architectural school circles, with their various brands of irony or self-indulgence, ran counter to the moral reminiscences of '68 radicalism, although both shared a dislike for established values.

Beyond such opposites lie the mythical shadows of Apollo's ethical and spiritual mindscapes versus Dionysius's erotic and sensual impulses. Architectural definitions, in their surgical precision, reinforce and amplify the impossible alternatives: on the one hand, architecture as a thing of the mind, a dematerialized or conceptual discipline with its typological and morphological variations, and on the other, architecture as an empirical event that concentrates on the senses, on the experience of space.

In the following paragraphs, I will attempt to show that today the pleasure of architecture may lie both inside *and* outside such oppositions—both in the dialectic *and* in the disintegration of the dialectic. However, the paradoxical nature of this theme is incompatible with the accepted, rational logic of classical argument; as Roland Barthes puts it in *The Pleasure of the Text:* "pleasure does not readily surrender to analysis," hence there will be no theses, antitheses, and syntheses here. The text instead is composed of fragments that relate only loosely to one another. These fragments—*geometry, mask, bondage, excess, eroticism*—are all to be considered not only within the reality of ideas but also within the reality of the reader's spatial experience: a silent reality that cannot be put on paper.

Fragment I   A Double Pleasure (Reminder)

The pleasure of space: This cannot be put into words, it is unspoken. Approximately: it is a form of experience—the "presence of absence"; exhilarating differences between the plane and the cavern, between the street and your living-room; symmetries and dissymmetries emphasizing the spatial properties of my body: right and left, up and down. Taken to its extreme, the pleasure of space leans toward the poetics of the unconscious, to the edge of madness.

The pleasure of geometry and, by extension, the pleasure of order—that is, the pleasure of concepts: Typical statements on architecture often read like the one in the first edition of the *Encyclopaedia Britannica* of 1773: "architecture, being governed by proportion, requires to be guided by rule and compass." That is, architecture is a "thing of the mind," a geometrical rather than a pictorial or experiential art, so the problem of architecture becomes a problem of ordinance—Doric or Corinthian order, axes or hierarchies, grids or regulating lines, types or models, walls or slabs—and, of course, the grammar and syntax of the architectures sign become pretexts for sophisticated and pleasurable manipulation. Taken to its extreme, such manipulation leans toward a poetic of frozen signs, detached from reality, into a subtle and frozen pleasure of the mind.

Neither the pleasure of space nor the pleasure of geometry is (on its own) the pleasure of architecture.

Fragment 2   Gardens of Pleasure

In his *Observations sur l'Architecture*, published in The Hague in 1765, Abbé Laugier suggested a dramatic deconstruction of architecture and its conventions. He wrote: "Whoever knows how to design a park well will have no difficulty in tracing the plan for the building of a city according to its given area and situation. There must be regularity and fantasy, relationships and oppositions, and casual, unexpected elements that vary the scene; great order in the details, confusion, uproar, and tumult in the whole."

Laugier's celebrated comments, together with the dreams of Capability Brown, William Kent, Lequeu, or Piranesi, were not merely a reaction to the Baroque period that preceded them. Rather, the deconstruction of architecture that they suggested was an early venture into the realm of pleasure, against the architectural order of time.

Take Stowe, for example. William Kent's park displays a subtle dialectic between organized landscape and architectural elements: the Egyptian pyramid, the Italian belvedere, the Saxon temple. But these "ruins" are to be read less as elements of a picturesque composition than as the dismantled elements of order. Yet, despite the apparent chaos, order is still present as a necessary counterpart to the sensuality of the winding streams. Without the signs of order,

Kent's park would lose all reminders of "reason." Conversely, without the traces of sensuality—trees, hedges, valleys—only symbols would remain, in a silent and frozen fashion.

Gardens have had a strange fate. Their history has almost always anticipated the history of cities. The orchard grid of man's earliest agricultural achievements preceded the layout of the first military cities. The perspectives and diagonals of the Renaissance garden were applied to the squares and colonnades of Renaissance cities. Similarly, the romantic, picturesque parks of English empiricism preempted the crescents and arcades of the rich urban-design tradition of nineteenth-century English cities.

Built exclusively for delight, gardens are like the earliest experiments in that part of architecture that is so difficult to express with words or drawings; pleasure and eroticism. Whether romantic or classical, gardens merge the sensual pleasure of space with the pleasure of reason, in a most *useless* manner.

Fragment 3　Pleasure and Necessity

"Uselessness" is associated only reluctantly with architectural matters. Even at a time when pleasure found some theoretical backing ("delight" as well as "commodity" and "firmness"), utility always provided a practical justification. One example among many is Quatremère de Quincy's introduction to the entry on architecture in the *Encyclopédie méthodique* published in Paris in 1778. There you will read a definition of architecture that contends that "amongst all the arts, those children of *pleasure and necessity*, with which man has formed a partnership in order to help him bear the pains of life and transmit his memory to future generations, it can certainly not be denied that architecture holds a most outstanding place. Considering it only from the point of view of *utility*, architecture surpasses all the arts. It provides for the salubrity of cities, guards the health of men, protects their property, and works only for the safety, repose and good order of civil life."

If De Quincy's statement was consistent with the architectural ideology of his time, then two hundred years later, the social necessity of architecture has been reduced to dreams and nostalgic utopias. The "salubrity of cities" is now determined more by the logic of land economics, while the "good order of civil life" is more often than not the order of corporate markets.

As a result, most architectural endeavors seem caught in a hopeless dilemma. If, on the one hand, architects recognize the ideological and financial dependency of their work, they implicitly accept the constraints of society. If, on the other hand, they sanctuarize themselves, their architecture is accused of elitism. Of course, architecture will save its peculiar nature, but only wherever it questions itself, wherever it denies or disrupts the form that a conservative society expects of it. Once again, if there has lately been some reason to doubt the necessity of architecture, then *the necessity of architecture may well be its non-necessity.* Such totally gratuitous consumption of architecture is ironically *political* in that it disturbs established structures. It is also pleasurable.

Fragment 4   Metaphor of Order–Bondage

Unlike the necessity of mere building, the non-necessity of architecture is undissociable from architectural histories, theories, and other precedents. These bonds enhance pleasure. The most excessive passion is always methodical. In such moments of intense desire, organization invades pleasure to such an extent that it is not always possible to distinguish the organizing constraints from the erotic matter. For example, the Marquis de Sade's heroes enjoyed confining their victims in the strictest convents before mistreating them according to rules carefully laid down with a precise and obsessive logic.

      Similarly, the game of architecture is an intricate play with rules that one may accept or reject. Indifferently called *système des Beaux-Arts* or modern movement precepts, this pervasive network of binding laws entangles architectural design. These rules, like so many knots that cannot be untied, are generally a paralyzing constraint. When manipulated, however, they have the erotic significance of bondage. To differentiate between rules or ropes is irrelevant here. What matters is that there is no simple bondage technique: the more numerous and sophisticated the restraints, the greater the pleasure.

Fragment 5 Rationality

In *Architecture and Utopia,* the historian Manfredo Tafuri recalls how the rational excesses of Piranesi's prisons took Laugier's theoretical proposals of "order and tumult" to the extreme. The classical vocabulary of architecture is Piranesi's chosen form of bondage. Treating classical elements as fragmented and decaying symbols, Piranesi's architecture battled against itself, in that the obsessive rationality of building types was "sadistically" carried to the extremes of irrationality.

Fragment 6 Eroticism

We have seen that the ambiguous pleasure of rationality and irrational dissolution recalled erotic concerns. A word of warning may be necessary at this stage. Eroticism is used here as a theoretical concept, having little in common with fetishistic formalism and other sexual analogies prompted by the sight of erect skyscrapers or curvaceous doorways. Rather, eroticism is a subtle matter. "The pleasure of excess" requires consciousness as well as voluptuousness. Neither space nor concepts alone are erotic, but the junction between the two is.

The ultimate pleasure of architecture is that impossible moment when an architectural act, brought to excess, reveals both the traces of reason and the immediate experience of space.

Fragment 7   Metaphor of Seduction—the Mask

There is rarely pleasure without seduction, or seduction without illusion. Consider: sometimes you wish to seduce, so you act in the most appropriate way in order to reach your ends. You wear a disguise. Conversely, you may wish to change roles and *be* seduced: you consent to someone else's disguise, you accept his or her assumed personality, for it gives you pleasure, even if you know that it dissimulates "something else."

Architecture is no different. It constantly plays the seducer. Its disguises are numerous: facades, arcades, squares, even architectural concepts become the artifacts of seduction. Like masks, they place a veil between what is assumed to be reality and its participants (you or I). So sometimes you desperately wish to read the reality behind the architectural mask. Soon, however, you realize that no single understanding is possible. Once you uncover that which lies behind the mask, it is only to discover another mask. The literal aspect of the disguise (the facade, the street) indicates other systems of knowledge, other ways to read the city: formal masks hide socioeconomic ones, while literal masks hide metaphorical ones. Each system of knowledge obscures another. Masks hide other masks, and each successive level of meaning confirms the impossibility of grasping reality.

Consciously aimed at seduction, masks are of course a category of reason. Yet they possess a double role: they simultaneously veil and unveil, simulate and dissimulate. Behind all masks lie dark and unconscious streams that cannot be dissociated from the pleasure of architecture. The mask may exalt appearances. Yet by its very presence, it says that, in the background, there is something else.

Fragment 8   Excess

If the mask belongs to the universe of pleasure, pleasure itself is no simple masquerade. The danger of confusing the mask with the face is real enough never to grant refuge to parodies and nostalgia. The need for order is no justification for imitating past orders. Architecture is interesting only when it masters the art of disturbing illusions, creating breaking points that can start and stop at any time.

Certainly, the pleasure of architecture is granted when architecture fulfills one's spatial expectations as well as embodies architectural ideas, concepts, or archetypes with intelligence, invention, sophistication, irony. Yet there is also a special pleasure that results from conflicts: when the sensual pleasure of space conflicts with the pleasure of order.

The recent widespread fascination with the history and theory of architecture does not necessarily mean a return to blind obedience to past dogma. On the contrary, I would suggest that the ultimate pleasure of architecture lies in the most forbidden parts of the architectural act; where limits are perverted and prohibitions are *transgressed*. The starting point of architecture is distortion—the dislocation of the universe that surrounds the architect. Yet such a nihilistic stance is only apparently so: we are not dealing with destruction here, but with excess, differences, and leftovers. *Exceeding* functionalist dogmas, semiotic systems, historical precedents, or formalized products of past social or economic constraints is not necessarily a matter of subversion but a matter of preserving the erotic capacity of architecture by disrupting the form that most conservative societies expect of it.

Fragment 9   Architecture of Pleasure

The architecture of pleasure lies where concept and experience of space abruptly coincide, where architectural fragments collide and merge in delight, where the culture of architecture is endlessly deconstructed and all rules are transgressed. No metaphorical paradise here, but discomfort and the unbalancing of expectations. Such architecture questions academic (and popular) assumptions, disturbs acquired tastes and fond architectural memories. Typologies, morphologies, spatial compressions, logical constructions—all dissolve. Such architecture is perverse because its real significance lies outside utility or purpose and ultimately is not even necessarily aimed at giving pleasure.

The architecture of pleasure depends on a particular feat, which is to keep architecture obsessed with itself in such an ambiguous fashion that it never surrenders to good conscience or parody, to debility or delirious neurosis.

Fragment 10   Advertisements for Architecture

There is no way to perform architecture in a book. Words and drawings can only produce paper space and not the experience of real space. By definition, paper space is imaginary: it is an image. Yet for those who do not build (whether for circumstantial or ideological reasons—it does not matter), it seems perfectly normal to be satisfied with the representation of those aspects of architecture that belong to mental constructs—to imagination. Such representations inevitably separate the sensual experience of a real space from the appreciation of rational concepts. Among other things, architecture is a function of both. And if either of these two criteria is removed, architecture loses something. It nevertheless seems strange that architects always have to castrate their architecture whenever they do not deal with real spaces. So the question remains: why should the paper space of a book or magazine replace an architectural space?

The answer does not lie in the inevitability of the media or in the way architecture is disseminated. Rather it may lie in the very nature of architecture.

Let's take an example. There are certain things that cannot be reached frontally. These things require analogies, metaphors, or roundabout routes in order to be grasped. For instance, it is through *language* that psychoanalysis uncovers the unconscious. Like a mask, language hints at something else behind itself. It may try to hide it, but it also implies it at the same time.

Architecture resembles a masked figure. It cannot easily be unveiled. It is always hiding: behind drawstrings, behind words, behind precepts, behind habits, behind technical constraints. Yet it is the very difficulty of uncovering architecture that makes it intensely desirable. This unveiling is part of the pleasure of architecture.

In a similar way, reality hides behind advertising. The usual function of advertisements—reproduced again and again, as opposed to the single architectural piece— is to trigger desire for something beyond the page itself. When removed from their customary endorsement of commodity values, advertisements are the ultimate magazine form, even if somehow ironically. And, as there are advertisements for architectural products, why not for the production (and reproduction) of *architecture*?

Fragment 10   Desire/Fragments

There are numerous ways to equate architecture with language. Yet such equations often amount to a *reduction* and an *exclusion*. A reduction, insofar as these equations usually become distorted as soon as architecture tries to produce meaning (which meaning? whose meaning?), and thus end up reducing language to its mere combinatory logic. An exclusion, insofar as these equations generally omit some of the important findings made in Vienna at the beginning of the century, when language was first seen as a condition of the unconscious. Here, dreams were analyzed as language as well as through language; language was called "the main street of the unconscious." Generally speaking, it appeared as a series of *fragments* (the Freudian notion of fragments does not presuppose the breaking of an image, or of a totality, but the dialectical multiplicity of a process).

So, too, architecture when equated with language can only be read as a series of fragments that make up an architectural reality.

Fragments of architecture (bits of walls, of rooms, of streets, of ideas) are all one actually sees. These fragments are like beginnings without ends. There is always a split between fragments that are real and fragments that are virtual, between memory and fantasy. These splits have no existence other than being the passage from one fragment to another. They are relays rather than signs. They are traces. They are in-between.

It is not the clash between these contradictory fragments that counts but the movement between them. And this invisible movement is neither a part of language nor of structure (*language* or *structure* are words specific to a mode of reading architecture that does not fully apply in the context of pleasure); it is nothing but a constant and mobile relationship inside language itself.

How such fragments are organized matters little: volume, height, surface, degree of enclosure, or whatever. These fragments are like sentences between quotation marks. Yet they are not quotations. They simply melt into the work. (We are here at the opposite of the collage technique.) They may be excerpts from different discourses, but this only demonstrates that an architectural project is precisely where differences find an overall expression.

An old film of the 1950s had a name for this movement between fragments. It was called desire. Yes, *A Streetcar Named Desire* perfectly simulated the movement toward something constantly missing, toward absence. Each setting, each fragment, was aimed at seduction but always dissolved at the moment it was approached. And then each time it would be substituted by another fragment. Desire was never seen. Yet it remained constant. The same goes for architecture.

In other words, architecture is not of interest because of its fragments and what they represent or do not represent. Nor does it consist in *exteriorizing*, through whatever forms, the unconscious desires of society or its architects. Nor is it a mere representation of those desires through some fantastic architectural image. Rather it can only act as a recipient in which your desires, my desires, can be reflected. Thus a piece of architecture is not architectural because it seduces, or because it fulfills some utilitarian function, but because it sets in motion the operations of seduction and the unconscious.

A word of warning. Architecture may very well activate such motions, but it is not a dream (a stage where society's or the individual's unconscious desires can be fulfilled). It cannot satisfy your wildest fantasies, but it may exceed the limits set by them.

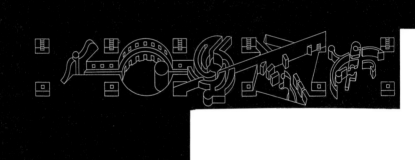

II Program | essays written between 1981 and 1983

To really appreciate architecture, you may even need to commit a murder.

Architecture is defined by the actions it witnesses
as much as by the enclosure of its walls. Murder
in the Street differs from Murder in the Cathedral
in the same way as love in the street differs from
the Street of Love. Radically.

Architecture and Limits

I.

In the work of remarkable writers, artists, or composers one sometimes finds disconcerting elements located at the edge of their production, at its limit. These elements, disturbing and out of character, are misfits within the artist's activity. Yet often such works reveal hidden codes and excesses hinting at other definitions, other interpretations.

The same can be said for whole fields of endeavor: there are productions at the limit of literature, at the limit of music, at the limit of theater. Such extreme positions inform us about the state of art, its paradoxes and its contradictions. These works, however, remain exceptions, for they seem dispensable—a luxury in the field of knowledge.

In architecture, such productions of the limit are not only historically frequent but indispensable: architecture simply does not exist without them. For example, architecture does not exist without drawing, in the same way that architecture does not exist without texts. Buildings have been erected without drawings, but architecture itself goes beyond the mere process of building. The complex cultural, social, and philosophical demands developed slowly over centuries have made architecture a form of knowledge in and of itself. Just as all forms of knowledge use different modes of discourse, so there are key architectural statements that, though not necessarily built, nevertheless inform us about the state of architecture—its concerns and its polemics—more precisely than the actual buildings of their time. Piranesi's engravings of prisons, Boullée's washes of monuments, have drastically influenced architectural thought and its related practice. The same could be said about particular architectural texts and theoretical positions. This does not exclude the built realm, for small constructions of an experimental nature have occasionally played a similar role.

Alternately celebrated and ignored, these works of the limit often provide isolated episodes amidst the mainstream of commercial production, for commerce cannot be ignored in a craft whose very scale involves cautious clients and carefully invested capital. Like the hidden clue in a detective story, these works are essential. In fact, the concept of limits is directly related to the very definition of architecture. What is meant by *to define*—"To determine the boundary or limits of," as well as "to set forth the essential nature of."[1]

Yet the current popularity of architectural polemics and the dissemination of its drawings in other domains have often masked these limits, restricting attention to the most obvious of architecture's aspects, curtailing it to a *Fountainhead* view of decorative heroics. By doing so, it reduces architectural concerns to a *dictionnaire des idées reçues*, dismissing less accessible works of an essential nature or, worse, distorting them through association with the mere necessities of a publicity market.

The present phenomenon is hardly new. The twentieth century contains numerous reductive policies aimed at mass media dissemination, to the extent that we now have two different versions of twentieth-century architecture. One, a maximalist version, aims at overall social, cultural, political, programmatic concerns while the other, minimalist, concentrates on sectors called style, technique, and so forth. But is it a question of choosing one over the other? Should one exclude the most rebellious and audacious projects, those of Melnikov or Poelzig for example, in the interest of preserving the stylistic coherence of the modern movement? Such exclusions, after all, are common architectural tactics. The modern movement had already started its attack on the beaux arts in the 1920s by a tactically belittling interpretation of nineteenth-century architecture. In the same way, the advocates of the International Style reduced the modern movement's radical concerns to homogenized iconographic mannerisms. Today, the most vocal representatives of architectural postmodernism use the same approach, but in reverse. By focusing their attack on the International Style, they make entertaining polemics and pungent journalism but offer little new to a cultural context that has long included the same historical allusions, ambiguous signs, and sensuousness they discover today.

Architectural thought is not a simple matter of opposing *Zeitgeist* to *Genius Loci*, conceptual concerns to allegorical ones, historical allusions to purist research. Unfortunately, architectural criticism remains an underdeveloped field. Despite its current popularity in the media, it generally belongs to the traditional genre, with "personality" profiles and "practicality" appraisals. Serious thematic critique is absent, except in the most specialized publications. Worse, critics there are partial to current reductive interpretations and often pretend that plurality of styles makes for complexity of thought. Thus it is not surprising that a solid critique of the current frivolity of architecture and architectural reporting hardly exists. "The bounds beyond which something ceases to be possible or allowable"[2] have been tightened to such an extent that we now witness a set of reductions highly damaging to the scope of the discipline. The narrowing of architecture as a form of knowledge into architecture as mere knowledge of form is matched only by the scaling down of generous research strategies into operational power broker tactics.

The current confusion becomes clear if one distinguishes, amidst current Venice or Paris Biennales, mass-market publications, and other public celebrations of architectural polemics, a worldwide battle between this narrow view of architectural history and research into the nature and definition of the discipline. The conflict is no mere dialectic but a real conflict corresponding, on a theoretical level, to practical battles that occur in everyday life within new commercial markets of architectural trivia, older corporate establishments, and ambitious university intelligentsia.

Modernism already contained such tactical battles and often hid them behind reductionist ideologies (formalism, functionalism, rationalism). The coherence these ideologies implied has revealed itself full of contradictions. Yet this is no reason to strip architecture again of its social, spatial, conceptual concerns and restrict its limits to a territory of "wit and irony," "conscious schizophrenia," "dual coding," and "twice-broken split-pediments."

Such reduction occurs in other, less obvious ways. The art world's fascination with architectural matters, evident in the obsessive number of "architectural reference" and "architectural sculpture" exhibitions, is well matched by the recent vogue among architects for advertising in reputable galleries. These works are useful only insofar as they inform us about the changing nature of the art. To envy architecture's usefulness or, reciprocally, to envy artists' freedom shows in both cases naiveté and misunderstanding of the work. Building may be about usefulness, architecture not necessarily so. To call architectural those sculptures that superficially borrow from a vocabulary of gables and stairs is as naive as to call paintings some architects' tepid water-colors or the P.R. renderings of commercial firms.

Such reciprocal envy is based on the narrow-est limits of outmoded interpretations, as if each discipline were inexorably drawn toward the other's most conservative texts. Yet the avant-garde of both fields sometimes enjoys a common sensibility, even if their terms of reference inevi-tably differ. It should be noted that architectural drawings, at their best, are a mode of working, of thinking about ar-chitecture. By their very nature, they usually refer to some-thing *outside* themselves (as opposed to those art drawings that refer only to themselves, to their own materiality and devices.)

But back to history. The pseudo-continuity of architectural history, with its neatly determined action-reaction episodes, is based on a poor understanding of history in general and architectural history in particular. After all, this history is not linear, and certain key productions are far from enslaved to artificial continuities. While mainstream historians have dismissed numerous works by qualifying them as "conceptual architecture," "cardboard architec-ture," "narrative" or "poetic" spaces, the time has come to systematically question their reductive strategies. Question-ing them is not purely a matter of celebrating what they reject. On the contrary, it means understanding what borderline activities hide and cover. This history, critique, and analysis remains to be done. Not as a fringe phenomenon (poets, visionaries or, worse, intellectuals) but as central to the *nature* of architecture.

II.

The limits of architecture are variable: each decade has its own ideal themes, its own confused fashions. Yet each of these periodical shifts and digressions raises the same question: are there recurrent themes, constants that are specifically architectural and yet always under scrutiny—an architecture of limits?

      As opposed to other disciplines, architecture rarely presents a coherent set of concepts—a definition—that displays both the continuity of its concerns and the more sensitive boundaries of its activity. However, a few aphorisms and dictums that have been transmitted through centuries of architectural literature do exist. Such notions as *scale, proportion, symmetry,* and *composition* have specific architectural connotations. The relation between the abstraction of thought and the substance of space—the Platonic distinction between *theoretical* and *practical*—is constantly recalled: to perceive the architectural space of a building is to perceive something-that-has-been-conceived. The opposition between form and function, between ideal types and programmatic organization, is similarly recurrent, even if both terms are viewed, increasingly, as independent.

One of the more enduring equations is the Vitruvian trilogy—*venustas, firmitas, utilitas*—"attractive appearance," "structural stability," "appropriate spatial accommodation." It is obsessively repeated throughout centuries of architectural precepts, though not necessarily in that order. Are these possible architectural constants, the inherent limits without which architecture does not exist? Or is their permanence a bad mental habit, an intellectual laziness observed throughout history? Does persistence grant validity? If not, does architecture fail to realize the displacement of limits it has held for so long?

The twentieth-century has disrupted the Vitruvian trilogy, for architecture could not remain insensitive to industrialization and the radical questioning of institutions (whether family, state, or church) at the turn of the century. The first term—attractive appearance (beauty)—slowly disappeared from the vocabulary, while structural linguistics took hold of the architect's formal discourse. Yet early architectural semiotics merely borrowed codes from literary texts, applied them to urban or architectural spaces, and inevitably remained descriptive. Inversely, attempts to construct new codes meant reducing a building to a "message" and its use to a "reading." Much of the current vogue for quotations of past architectural symbols proceeds from such simplistic interpretations.

In recent years, however, serious research has applied linguistic theory to architecture, adding an arsenal of selection and combination, substitution and contextuality, metaphor and metonymy, similarity and contiguity, following the terms of Jakobson, Chomsky, and Benveniste. Although exclusively formalist manipulation often exhausts itself if new criteria are not injected to allow for innovation, its very excesses can often shed new light on the elusive boundaries of the "prison-house" of architectural language. At the limit, this research introduces preoccupations with the notion of subject and with the role of subjectivity in language, differentiating language as a system of signs from language as an act accomplished by an individual.

The concern for the next term—structural stability—seems to have disappeared during the 1960s without anyone realizing or discussing it. The consensus was that anything could be built, provided you could pay for it. And concern with structure vanished from conference rosters and dwindled in architectural courses and magazines. Who, after all, wants to stress that the Doric pilasters of current historicism are made of painted plywood or that appliqué moldings are there to give metaphorical substance to hollow walls?

In the 1980s, interest in engineering issues returned but was often marked by a particular condition: the progressive reduction of building mass over a period of centuries meant that architects could arbitrarily compose, decompose, and recompose volumes according to formal rather than structural laws. Modernism's concern for surface effect further deprived volumes of material substance. Today, matter hardly enters the substance of walls that have been reduced to sheetrock or glass partitions that barely differentiate inside from outside. The phenomenon is not likely to be reversed, and those who advocate a return to "honesty of materials" or massive poché walls are often motivated by ideological rather than practical reasons. It should be stressed, however, that any concern over material substance has implications beyond mere structural stability. The materiality of architecture, after all, is in its solids and voids, its spatial sequences, its articulations, its collisions. (One remark in passing: some will say concern for energy conservation replaced the concern for construction. Maybe. Research in passive and active energy conservation, solar power, and water recycling certainly enjoys a distinct popularity yet does not greatly affect the general vocabulary of houses or cities.)

The sole judge of the last term of the trilogy, "appropriate spatial accommodation" is, of course, the body, your body, my body—the starting point and point of arrival of architecture. The Cartesian body-as-object has been opposed to the phenomenological body-as-subject, and the materiality and logic of the body has been opposed to the materiality and logic of spaces. From the space of the body to the body-in-space—the passage is intricate. And that shift, that gap in the obscurity of the unconscious, somewhere between body and Ego, between Ego and Other. . . . Architecture still has not begun to analyze the Viennese discoveries at the turn of the century, even if architecture might one day inform psychoanalysis more than psychoanalysis has informed architecture.

The pervasive smells of rubber, concrete, flesh; the taste of dust; the discomforting rubbing of an elbow on an abrasive surface; the pleasure of fur-lined walls and the pain of a corner hit upon in the dark; the echo of a hall—space is not simply the three-dimensional projection of a mental representation, but it is something that is heard, and is acted upon. And it is the eye that frames—the window, the door, the vanishing ritual of passage. . . . Spaces of movement—corridors, staircases, ramps, passages, thresholds; here begins the articulation between the space of the senses and the space of society, the dances and gestures that combine the representation of space and the space of representation. Bodies not only move in but generate spaces produced by and through their movements. Movements—of dance, sport, war—are the intrusion of events into architectural spaces. At the limit, these events become scenarios or programs, void of moral or functional implications, independent but inseparable from the spaces that enclose them.

So a new formulation of the old trilogy appears. It overlaps the three original terms in certain ways while enlarging them in other ways. Distinctions can be made between mental, physical, and social space or, alternatively, between language, matter, and body. Admittedly, these distinctions are schematic. Although they correspond to real and convenient categories of analysis ("conceived," "perceived," "experienced"), they lead to different approaches and to different modes of architectural notation.

A change is evident in architecture's status, in its relationship to its language, its composing materials, and its individuals or societies. The question is how these three terms are articulated and how they relate to each other within the field of contemporary practice. It is also evident that since architecture's mode of production has reached an advanced stage of development, it no longer needs to adhere strictly to linguistic, material, or functional norms but can distort them at will. And, finally, it is evident from the role of isolated incidents—often pushed aside in the past—that architecture's nature is not always found within building. Events, drawings, texts expand the boundaries of socially justifiable constructions.

The recent changes are deep and little understood. Architects-at-large find them difficult to accept, intuitively aware as they are that their craft is being drastically altered. Current architectural historicism is both a part of and a consequence of this phenomenon—both a sign of fear and a sign of escape. To what extent do such explosions, such changes in the conditions of the production of architecture *displace the limits* of architectural activities in order to correspond to their mutations?

III.

Program: a descriptive notice, issued beforehand, of any formal series of proceedings, as a festive celebration, a course of study etc. (. . .), a list of the items or "numbers" of a concert etc., in the order of performance; hence the items themselves collectively, the performance as a whole. . . .[3]

An architectural program is a list of required utilities; it indicates their relations, but suggests neither their combination nor their proportion.[4]

To address the notion of the program today is to enter a forbidden field, a field architectural ideologies have consciously banished for decades. Programmatic concerns have been dismissed both as remnants of humanism and as morbid attempts to resurrect now-obsolete functionalist doctrines. These attacks are revealing in that they imply an embedded belief in one particular aspect of modernism—the preeminence of formal manipulation to the exclusion of social or utilitarian considerations, a preeminence that even current postmodernist architecture has refused to challenge.

But let us briefly recall some historical facts that govern the notion of the program. Although the eighteenth century's development of scientific techniques based on spatial and structural analysis had already led architectural theorists to consider use and construction as separate disciplines, and hence to stress pure formal manipulation, the program long remained an important part of the architectural process. Implicitly or explicitly related to the needs of the period or the state, the program's apparently objective requirements by and large reflected particular cultures and values. This was true of the beaux arts' "Stables for a Sovereign Prince" of 1739 and the "Public Festival for the Marriage of a Prince" of 1769. Growing industrialization and urbanization soon generated their own programs. Department stores, railway stations, and arcades were nineteenth-century programs born of commerce and industry. Usually complex, they did not readily result in precise forms, and mediating factors like ideal buildings types were often required, risking a complete disjunction between "form" and "content."

The modern movement's early attacks on the empty formulas of academicism condemned these disjunctions, along with the decadent content of most beaux arts programs, which were regarded as pretexts for repetitive compositional recipes. The concept of the program itself was not attacked, but, rather, the way it reflected an obsolete society. Instead, closer links between new social contents, technologies, and pure geometries announced a new functionalist ethic. At the first level, this ethic emphasized problem solving rather than problem formulating: good architecture was to grow from the objective problem peculiar to building, site, and client, in an organic or mechanical manner. On a second and more heroic level, the revolutionary urges of the futurist and constructivist avant-gardes joined those of early nineteenth-century utopian social thinkers to create new programs. "Social condensers," communal kitchens, workers' clubs, theaters, factories, or even *unités d'habitation* accompanied a new vision of social and family structure. In a frequently naive manner, architecture was meant to both reflect and mold the society to come.

Yet by the early 1930s in the United States and Europe, a changing social context favored new forms and technologies at the expense of programmatic concerns. By the 1950s modern architecture had been emptied of its early ideological basis, partially due to the virtual failure of its utopian aims. Architecture also found a new base in the theories of modernism developed in literature, art, and music. "Form follows form" replaced "form follows function," and soon attacks on functionalism were voiced by neo-modernists for ideological reasons, and by postmodernists for esthetic ones.

In any case, enough programs managed to function in buildings conceived for entirely different purposes to prove the simple point that there was no necessary causal relationship between function and subsequent form, or between a given building type and a given use. Among confirmed modernists, the more conventional the program, the better; conventional programs, with their easy solutions, left room for experimentation in style and language, much as Karl Heinz Stockhausen used national anthems as the material for syntactical transformations.

The academization of constructivism, the influence of literary formalism, and the example of modernist painting and sculpture all contributed to architecture's reduction to simple linguistic components. When applied to architecture, Clement Greenberg's dictum that content be "dissolved so completely into form that the work of art or literature cannot be reduced in whole or in part to anything but itself . . . subject matter or content becomes something to be avoided like a plague" further removed considerations of use. Ultimately, in the 1970s, mainstream modernist criticism, by focusing on the intrinsic qualities of autonomous objects, formed an alliance with semiotic theory to make architecture an easy object of poetics.

But wasn't architecture different from painting or literature? Could use or program be part of form rather than a subject or content? Didn't Russian formalism differ from Greenbergian modernism in that, rather than banishing considerations of content, it simply no longer opposed form to content but began to conceive of it as the *totality* of the work's various components? Content could be equally formal.

Much of the theory of architectural modernism (which, notably, emerged in the 1950s rather than in the 1920s) was similar to all modernism in its search for the specificity of architecture, for that which is characteristic of architecture alone. But how was such specificity defined? Did it include or exclude use? It is significant that architectural postmodernism's challenge to the linguistic choices of modernism has never assaulted its value system. To discuss "the crisis of architecture" in wholly stylistic terms was a false polemic, a clever feint aimed at masking the absence of concerns about use.

While it is not irrelevant to distinguish between an autonomous, self-referential architecture that transcends history and culture and an architecture that echoes historical or cultural precedents and regional contexts, it should be noted that both address the same definition of architecture as formal or stylistic manipulation. Form still follows form; only the meaning and the frame of reference differ. Beyond their diverging esthetic means, both conceive of architecture as an object of contemplation, easily accessible to critical attention, as opposed to the interaction of space and events, which is usually unremarked upon. Thus walls and gestures, columns and figures are rarely seen as part of a single signifying system. Theories of reading, when applied to architecture, are largely fruitless in that they reduce it to an art of communication or to a visual art (the so-called single-coding of modernism, or the double-coding of postmodernism), dismissing the "intertextuality" that makes architecture a highly complex human activity. The multiplicity of heterogeneous discourses, the constant interaction between movement, sensual experience, and conceptual acrobatics refute the parallel with the visual arts.

If we are to observe, today, an epistemological break with what is generally called modernism, then it must also question its own formal contingency. By no means does this imply a return to notions of function versus form, to cause-and-effect relationships between program and type, to utopian visions, or to the varied positivist or mechanistic ideologies of the past. On the contrary, it means going beyond reductive interpretations of architecture. The usual exclusion of the body and its experience from all discourse on the logic of form in a case in point.

The mise-en-scènes of Peter Behrens, who organized ceremonies amidst the spaces of Josef Maria Olbrich's *Mathildenhoehe*; Hans Poelzig's sets for *The Golem*; Laszlo Moholy-Nagy's stage designs, which combined cinema, music, sets, and actions, freezing simultaneities; El

Lissitzky's displays of electromechanical acrobatics; Oskar Schlemmer's gestural dances; and Konstantin Melnikov's "Montage of Attractions," which turned into real architectural constructions—all exploded the restrictive orthodoxy of architectural modernism. There were, of course, precedents—Renaissance pageants, Jacques Louis David's revolutionary fêtes, and, later and more sinister, Albert Speer's Cathedral of Ice and the Nuremberg Rally.

More recently, departures from formal discourses and renewed concerns for architectural events have taken an imaginary programmatic mode.[5] Alternatively, typological studies have begun to discuss the critical "affect" of ideal building types that were historically born of function but were later displaced into new programs alien to their original purpose. These concerns for events, ceremonies, and programs suggest a possible distance vis-à-vis both modernist orthodoxy and historicist revival.

1–3.

Violence of Architecture ▬

1. *There is no architecture without action, no architecture without events, no architecture without program.*

2. *By extension, there is no architecture without violence.*

The first of these statements runs against the mainstream of architectural thought by refusing to favor space at the expense of action. The second statement argues that although the logic of objects and the logic of man are independent in their relations to the world, they inevitably face one another in an intense confrontation. Any relationship between a building and its users is one of violence, for any use means the intrusion of a human body into a given space, the intrusion of one order into another. This intrusion is inherent in the idea of architecture; any reduction of architecture to its spaces at the expense of its events is as simplistic as the reduction of architecture to its facades.

By "violence," I do not mean the brutality that destroys physical or emotional integrity but a metaphor for the intensity of a relationship between individuals and their surrounding spaces. The argument is not a matter of style: modern architecture is neither more or less violent than classical architecture, or than fascist, socialist, or vernacular variations. Architecture's violence is fundamental and unavoidable, for architecture is linked to events in the same way that the guard is linked to the prisoner, the police to the criminal, the doctor to the patient, order to chaos. This also suggests that actions qualify spaces as much as spaces qualify actions; that space and action are inseparable and that no proper interpretation of architecture, drawing, or notation can refuse to consider this fact.

What must first be determined is whether this relation between action and space is symmetrical—opposing two camps (people versus spaces) that affect one another in a comparable way—or asymmetrical, a relation in which one camp, whether space or people, clearly dominates the other.

Bodies Violating Space

First, there is the violence that all individuals inflict on spaces by their very presence, by their intrusion into the controlled order of architecture. Entering a building may be a delicate act, but it violates the balance of a precisely ordered geometry (do architectural photographs ever include runners, fighters, lovers?). Bodies carve all sorts of new and unexpected spaces, through fluid or erratic motions. Architecture, then, is only an organism engaged in constant intercourse with users, whose bodies rush against the carefully established rules of architectural thought. No wonder the human body has always been suspect in architecture: it has always set limits to the most extreme architectural ambitions. The body disturbs the purity of architectural order. It is equivalent to a dangerous prohibition.

Violence is not always present. Just as riots, brawls, insurrections, and revolutions are of limited duration, so is the violence a body commits against space. Yet it is always implicit. Each door implies the movement of someone crossing its frame. Each corridor implies the progression of movement that blocks it. Each architectural space implies (and desires) the intruding presence that will inhabit it.

Space Violating Bodies

But if bodies violate the purity of architectural spaces, one might rightly wonder about the reverse: the violence inflicted by narrow corridors on large crowds, the symbolic or physical violence of buildings on users. A word of warning: I do not wish to resurrect recent behaviorist architectural approaches. Instead, I wish simply to underline the mere existence of a physical presence and the fact that it begins quite innocently, in an *imaginary* sort of way.

The place your body inhabits is inscribed in your imagination, your unconscious, as a space of possible bliss. Or menace. What if you are forced to abandon your imaginary spatial markings? A torturer wants you, the victim, to regress, because he wants to demean his prey, to make you lose your identity as a subject. Suddenly you have no choice; running away is impossible. The rooms are too small or too big, the ceilings too low or too high. Violence exercised by and through space is spatial torture.

Take Palladio's Villa Rotonda. You walk through one of its axes, and as you cross the central space and reach its other side you find, instead of the hillside landscape, the steps of another Villa Rotonda, and another, and another, and another. The incessant repetition at first stimulates some strange desire, but soon becomes sadistic, impossible, violent.

Such discomforting spatial devices can take any form: the white anechoic chambers of sensory deprivation, the formless spaces leading to psychological destructuring. Steep and dangerous staircases, those corridors consciously made too narrow for crowds, introduce a radical shift from architecture as an object of contemplation to architecture as a perverse instrument of use. At the same time it must be stressed that the receiving subject—you or I—may wish to be subjected to such spatial aggression, just as you may go to a rock concert and stand close enough to the loudspeakers to sustain painful—but pleasurable—physical or psychic trauma. Places aimed at the cult of excessive sound only suggest places aimed at the cult of excessive space. The love of violence, after all, is an ancient pleasure.

Why has architectural theory regularly refused to acknowledge such pleasures and always claimed (at least officially) that architecture should be pleasing to the eye, as well as comfortable to the body? This presupposition seems curious when the pleasure of violence can be experienced in every other human activity, from the violence of discordant sounds in music to the clash of bodies in sports, from gangster movies to the Marquis de Sade.

Violence Ritualized

Who will mastermind these exquisite spatial delights, these disturbing architectural tortures, the tortuous paths of promenades through delirious landscapes, theatrical events where actor complements decor? Who . . .? The architect? By the seventeenth century, Bernini had staged whole spectacles, followed by Mansart's fêtes for Louis XIV and Albert Speer's sinister and beautiful rallies. After all, the original action, the original act of violence—this unspeakable copulating of live body and dead stone—is unique and unrehearsed, though perhaps infinitely repeatable, for you may enter the building again and again. The architect will always dream of purifying this uncontrolled violence, channeling obedient bodies along predictable paths and occasionally along ramps that provide striking vistas, ritualizing the transgression of bodies in space. Le Corbusier's Carpenter Center, with its ramp that violates the building, is a genuine movement of bodies made into an architectural solid. Or the reverse: it is a solid that forcibly channels the movement of bodies.

The original, spontaneous interaction of the body with a space is often purified by ritual. Sixteenth-century pageants and Nathan Altman's reenactment of the storming of the Winter Palace in St. Petersburg, for example, are ritualistic imitations of spontaneous violence. Endlessly repeated, these rituals curb all aspects of the original act that have escaped control: the choice of time and place, the selection of the victim. . . .

A ritual implies a near-frozen relationship between action and space. It institutes a new order after the disorder of the original event. When it becomes necessary to mediate tension and fix it by custom, then no single fragment must escape attention. Nothing strange and unexpected must happen. Control must be absolute.

Programs: Reciprocity and Conflict

Such control is, of course, not likely to be achieved. Few regimes would survive if architects were to program every single movement of individual and society in a kind of ballet mécanique of architecture, a permanent Nuremberg Rally of everyday life, a puppet theater of spatial intimacy. Nor would they survive if every spontaneous movement were immediately frozen into a solid corridor. The relationship is more subtle and moves beyond the question of power, beyond the question of whether architecture dominates events or vice versa. The relationship, then, is as symmetrical as the ineluctable one between guard and prisoner, hunter and hunted. But both the hunter and the hunted also have basic needs to consider, which may not relate to the hunt: sustenance, food, shelter, and so forth. Hunter and hunted enjoy these needs independent of the fact that they are engaged in a deadly game. They are respectively self-sufficient. Only when they confront each other's reality are their strategies so totally interdependent that it becomes impossible to determine which one initiates and which one responds. The same happens with architecture and the way buildings relate to their users, or spaces relate to events or programs. For any organized repetition of events, once announced in advance, becomes a program, a descriptive notice of a formal series of proceedings.

When spaces and programs are largely independent of one another, one observes a strategy of indifference in which architectural considerations do not depend on utilitarian ones, in which space has one logic and events another. Such were the Crystal Palace and the neutral sheds of the nineteenth-century's Great Exhibitions, which accommodated anything from displays of elephants draped in rare colonial silks to international boxing matches. Such, too— but in a very different manner—was Gerrit Rietveld's house in Utrecht, a remarkable exercise in architectural language, and a not unpleasant house to live in, despite, or perhaps because of the fortuitous juxtaposition of space and use.

At other times, architectural spaces and programs can become totally interdependent and fully condition each other's existence. In these cases, the architect's view of the user's needs determines every architectural decision (which may, in turn, determine the user's attitude). The architect designs the set, writes the script, and directs the actors. Such were the ideal kitchen installations of the twenties' Werkbund, each step of a near-biochemical housewife carefully monitored by the design's constant attention. Such were Meyerhold's biomechanics, acting through Popova's stage sets, where the characters' logic played with and against the logic of their dynamic surroundings. Such also is Frank Lloyd Wright's Guggenheim Museum. It is not a question of knowing which comes first, movement or space, which molds the other, for ultimately a deep bond is involved. After all, they are caught in the same set of relationships; only the arrow of power changes direction.

(If I outline these two relations of independence and interdependence, it is to insist on the fact that they exist regardless of the prescriptive ideologies—modernism versus humanism, formalism versus functionalism, and so on—which architects and critics are usually keen to promote.)

Most relations, of course, stand somewhere in between. You can sleep in your kitchen. And fight and love. These shifts are not without meaning. When the typology of an eighteenth-century prison is turned into a twentieth-century city hall, the shift inevitably suggests a critical statement about institutions. When an industrial loft in

4–7.

Manhattan is turned into a residence, a similar shift occurs, a shift that is undoubtedly less dramatic. Spaces are qualified by actions just as actions are qualified by spaces. One does not trigger the other; they exist independently. Only when they intersect do they affect one another. Remember Kuleshov's experiment where the same shot of the actor's impassive face is introduced into a variety of situations, and the audience reads different expressions into each successive juxtaposition. The same occurs in architecture: the event is altered by each new space. And vice versa: by ascribing to a given, supposedly "autonomous" space a contradictory program, the space attains new levels of meaning. Event and space do not merge but affect one another. Similarly if the Sistine Chapel were used for pole-vaulting events, architecture would then cease to yield to its customary good intentions. For a while the transgression would be real and all-powerful. Yet the transgression of cultural expectations soon becomes accepted. Just as violent surrealist collages inspire advertising rhetoric, the broken rule is integrated into everyday life, whether through symbolic or technological motivations.

If violence is the key metaphor for the intensity of a relationship, then the very physicality of architecture transcends the metaphor. There is a deep sensuality, an unremittent eroticism in architecture. Its underlying violence varies according to the forces that are put into play—rational forces, irrational forces. They can be deficient or excessive. Little activity—hypoactivity—in a house can be as disturbing as hyperactivity. Asceticism and orgiastic excesses are closer

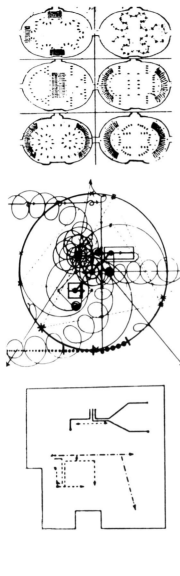

than architectural theorists have admitted, and the asceticism of Gerrit Rietveld's or Ludwig Wittgenstein's house inevitably implies the most extreme bacchanals. (Cultural expectations merely affect the perception of violence, but do not alter its nature: slapping your lover's face is perceived differently from culture to culture.)

Architecture and events constantly transgress each other's rules, whether explicitly or implicitly. These rules, these organized compositions, may be questioned, but they always remain points of reference. A building is a point of reference for the activities set to negate it. A theory of architecture is a theory of order threatened by the very use it permits. And vice versa.

The integration of the concept of violence into the architectural mechanism—the purpose of my argument—is ultimately aimed at a new pleasure of architecture. Like any form of violence, the violence of architecture also contains the possibility of change, of renewal. Like any violence, the violence of architecture is deeply Dionysian. It should be understood, and its contradictions maintained in a dynamic manner, with their conflicts and complementarity.

In passing, two types of partial violence should be distinguished, types which are *not* specifically architectural. The first is *formal violence,* which deals with the conflicts between objects. Such is the violence of form versus form, the violence of Giovanni Battista Piranesi's juxtapositions, Kurt Schwitters' Merzbau collages, and other architectural collisions. Distortions, ruptures, compressions, fragmentations, and disjunctions are inherent in the

12–14.

Violence of Architecture

manipulation of form. This is also the disruption inflicted by any new construction on its surroundings, for it not only destroys what it replaces but also violates the territory it occupies. It is the violence of Adolf Loos's House for Tristan Tzara in the context of vernacular nineteenth-century sub-urban Paris or, alternatively, the disruptive effect of an his-torical allusion in a curtain-wall avenue. This contextual violence is nothing but the polemical violence of difference. To discuss it is the task of sociology, psychology, and esthetics.

A door flanked by broken Corinthian col-umns supporting a twisted neon pediment, however, sug-gests farce rather than violence. Yet James Joyce's "door-lumn" was both a pun and a comment on the cultural crisis of language. *Finnegans Wake* implied that particular transgressions could attack the constituent elements of ar-chitectural language—its columns, stairs, windows, and their various combinations—as they are defined by any cul-tural period, whether beaux arts or Bauhaus. This formal disobedience is ultimately harmless and may even initiate a new style as it slowly loses the excessive character of a violated prohibition. It then announces a new pleasure and the elaboration of a new norm, which is in turn violated.

The second type of partial violence is not a metaphor. *Programmatic violence* encompasses those uses, actions, events, and programs that, by accident or by design, are specifically evil and destructive. Among them are killing, internment, and torture, which become slaughterhouses, concentration camps, or torture chambers.

15–18.

19.

Paul Wegener, *Der Golem,* 1920. Set by Hans Poelzig.

Spaces and Events

                                                                                            ▬

Can one attempt to make a contribution to architectural discourse by relentlessly stating that there is no space without event, no architecture without program? This seems to be our mandate at a time that has witnessed the revival of historicism or, alternatively, of formalism in almost every architectural circle. Our work argues that architecture—its social relevance and formal invention—cannot be dissociated from the events that "happen" in it. Recent projects insist constantly on issues of program and notation. They stress a critical attitude that observes, analyzes, and interprets some of the most controversial positions of past and present architectural ideologies.

Yet this work often took place against the mainstream of the prevalent architectural discourse. For throughout the 1970s there was an exacerbation of stylistic concerns at the expense of programmatic ones and a reduction of architecture as a form of knowledge to architecture as knowledge of form. From modernism to postmodernism, the history of architecture was surreptitiously turned into a history of styles. This perverted form of history borrowed from semiotics the ability to "read" layers of interpretation but reduced architecture to a system of surface signs at the expense of the reciprocal, indifferent, or even conflictive relationship of spaces and events.

This is not the place for an extensive analysis of the situation that engulfed the critical establishment. However, it should be stressed that it is no accident that this emphasis on stylistic issues corresponded to a double and wider phenomenon: on the one hand, the increasing role of the developer in planning large buildings, encouraging many architects to become mere decorators, and on the other, the tendency of many architectural critics to concentrate on surface readings, signs, metaphors, and other modes of presentation, often to the exclusion of spatial or programmatic concerns. These are two faces of a single coin, typical of an increasing desertion by the architectural profession of its responsibilities vis-à-vis the events and activities that take place in the spaces it designs.

At the start of the 1980s, the notion of program was still forbidden territory. Programatic concerns were rejected as leftovers from obsolete functionalist doctrines by those polemicists who saw programs as mere pretexts for stylistic experimentation. Few dared to explore the relation between the formal elaboration of spaces and the invention of programs, between the abstraction of architectural thought and the representation of events. The popular dissemination of architectural images through eye-catching reproductions in magazines often turned architecture into a passive object of contemplation instead of the *place* that confronts spaces and actions. Most exhibitions of architecture in art galleries and museums encouraged "surface" practice and presented the architect's work as a form of decorative painting. Walls and bodies, abstract planes and figures were rarely seen as part of a single signifying system. History may one day look upon this period as the moment of the loss of innocence in twentieth-century architecture: the moment when it became clear that neither supertechnology, expressionist functionalism, nor neo-Corbusianism could solve society's ills and that architecture was not ideologically neutral. A strong political upheaval, a rebirth of critical thought in architecture, and new developments in history and theory all triggered a phenomenon whose consequences are still unmeasured. This general loss of innocence resulted in a variety of moves by architects according to their political or ideological leanings. In the early 1970s, some denounced architecture altogether, arguing that its practice, in the current socioeconomic context, could only be reactionary and reinforce the status quo. Others, influenced by structural linguistics, talked of "constants" and the rational autonomy of an architecture that transcended all social forms. Others reintroduced political discourse and advocated a return to preindustrial forms of society. And still others cynically took the analyses of style and ideology by Barthes, Eco, or Baudrillard and diverted them from their critical aims, turning them over like a glove. Instead of using them to question the distorted, mediated nature of architectural practice, these architects injected meaning into their buildings artificially, through a collage of historicist or metaphorical elements. The restricted notion of postmodernism that ensued—a notion diminished by comparison with literature or art—completely and uncritically reinserted architecture into the cycle of consumption.

At the Architectural Association (AA) in London, I devised a program entitled "Theory, Language, Attitudes." Exploiting the structure of the AA, which encouraged autonomous research and independent lecture courses, it played on an opposition between political and theoretical concerns about the city (those of Baudrillard, Lefèbvre, Adorno, Lukács, and Benjamin, for example) and an art sensibility informed by photography, conceptual art, and performance. This opposition between a verbal critical discourse and a visual one suggested that the two were complementary. Students' projects explored that overlapping sensibility, often in a manner sufficiently obscure to generate initial hostility through the school. Of course the codes used in the students' work differed sharply from those seen in schools and architectural offices at the time. At the end-of-year exhibition texts, tapes, films, manifestos, rows of storyboards, and photographs of ghostlike figures, each with their own specific conventions, intruded in a space arranged according to codes disparate from those of the profession.

Photography was used obsessively: as "live" insert, as artificial documentation, as a hint of reality interposed in architectural drawing—a reality nevertheless distanced and often manipulated, filled with skillful staging, with characters and sets in their complementary relations. Students enacted fictitious programs inside carefully selected "real" spaces and then shot entire photographic sequences as evidence of their architectural endeavors. Any new attitude to architecture *had* to question its mode of representation.

Other works dealing with a critical analysis of urban life were generally in written form. They were turned into a book, edited, designed, printed, and published by the unit; hence, "the words of architecture became the work of architecture," as we said. Entitled *A Chronicle of Urban Politics,* the book attempted to analyze what distinguished our period from the preceding one. Texts on fragmentation, cultural dequalification, and the "intermediate city" analyzed consumerism, totems, and representationalism. Some of the texts announced, several years in advance, preoccupations now common to the cultural sphere: dislo-

Untitled photo collage, *Harper and Queen,* c. 1971.

cated imagery, artificiality, representational reality versus experienced reality.

The mixing of genres and disciplines in this work was widely attacked by the academic establishment, still obsessed with concepts of disciplinary autonomy and self-referentiality. But the significance of such events is not a matter of historical precedence or provocation. In superimposing ideas and perceptions, words and spaces, these events underlined the importance of a certain kind of relationship between abstraction and narrative—a complex juxtaposition of abstract concepts and immediate experiences, contradictions, superimpositions of mutually exclusive sensibilities. This dialectic between the verbal and the visual culminated in 1974 in a series of "literary" projects organized in the studio, in which texts provided programs or events on which students were to develop architectural works. The role of the text was fundamental in that it underlined some aspect of the complementing (or, occasionally, lack of complementing) of events and spaces. Some texts, like Italo Calvino's metaphorical descriptions of "Invisible Cities," were so "architectural" as to require going far beyond the mere illustration of the author's already powerful descriptions; Franz Kafka's *Burrow* challenged conventional architectural perceptions and modes of representation; Edgar Allan Poe's *Masque of the Red Death* (done during my term as Visiting Critic at Princeton University) suggested parallels between narrative and spatial sequences. Such explorations of the intricacies of language and space naturally had to touch on James Joyce's discoveries. During one of my trips from the

United States I gave extracts from *Finnegans Wake* as the program. The site was London's Covent Garden and the architecture was derived, by analogy or opposition, from Joyce's text. The effect of such research was invaluable in providing a framework for the analysis of the relations between events and spaces, beyond functionalist notions.

The unfolding of events in a literary context inevitably suggested parallels to the unfolding of events in architecture.

Space versus Program

To what extent could the literary narrative shed light on the organization of events in buildings, whether called "use," "functions," "activities," or "programs"? If writers could manipulate the structure of stories in the same way as they twist vocabulary and grammar, couldn't architects do the same, organizing the program in a similarly objective, detached, or imaginative way? For if architects could self-consciously use such devices as repetition, distortion, or juxtaposition in the formal elaboration of walls, couldn't they do the same thing in terms of the activities that occurred within those very walls? Pole vaulting in the chapel, bicycling in the laundromat, sky diving in the elevator shaft? Raising these questions proved increasingly stimulating: conventional organizations of spaces could be matched to the most surrealistically absurd sets of activities. Or vice versa: the most intricate and perverse organization of spaces could accommodate the everyday life of an average suburban family.

Such research was obviously not aimed at providing immediate answers, whether ideological or practical. Far more important was the understanding that the relation between program and building could be either highly sympathetic or contrived and artificial. The latter, of course, fascinated us more, as it rejected all functionalist leanings. It was a time when most architects were questioning, attacking, or outright rejecting modern movement orthodoxy. We simply refused to enter these polemics, viewing them as stylistic or semantic battles. Moreover, if this orthodoxy was often attacked for its reduction to minimalist formal manipulations, we refused to enrich it with witty metaphors. Issues of intertextuality, multiple readings and dual codings had to integrate the notion of program. To use a Palladian arch for an athletic club alters both Palladio and the nature of the athletic event.

As an exploration of the disjunction between expected form and expected use, we began a series of projects opposing specific programs with particular, often conflicting spaces. Programatic context versus urban typology, urban typology versus spatial experience, spatial experience versus procedure, and so on, provided a dialectical framework for research. We consciously suggested programs that were impossible on the sites that were to house them: a stadium in Soho, a prison near Wardour Street, a ballroom in a churchyard. At the same time, issues of *notation* became fundamental: if the reading of architecture was to include the events that took place in it, it would be necessary to devise modes of notating such activities. Several modes of notation were invented to supplement the limitations of plans, sections, or axonometrics. Movement notation derived from choreography, and simultaneous scores derived from music notation were elaborated for architectural purposes.

If movement notation usually proceeded from our desire to map the actual movement of bodies in spaces, it increasingly became a sign that did not necessarily refer to these movements but rather to the *idea* of movement—a form of notation that was there to *recall* that architecture was also about the movement of bodies in space, that their language and the language of walls were ultimately complementary. Using movement notation as a means of recalling issues was an attempt to include new and stereotypical codes in architectural drawing and, by extension, in its perception; layerings, juxtaposition, and superimposition of images purposefully blurred the conventional relationship between plan, graphic conventions and their meaning in the built realm. Increasingly the drawings became both the notation of a complex architectural reality *and* drawings (art works) in their own right, with their own frame of reference, deliberately set apart from the conventions of architectural plans and sections.

The fascination with the dramatic, either in the program (murder, sexuality, violence) or in the mode of representation (strongly outlined images, distorted angles of vision—as if seen from a diving airforce bomber), is there to force a response. Architecture ceases to be a backdrop for actions, becoming the action itself.

All this suggests that "shock" must be manufactured by the architect if architecture is to communicate. Influence from the mass media, from fashion and popular magazines, informed the choice of programs: the lunatic asylum, the fashion institute, the Falklands war. It also influenced the graphic techniques, from the straight black and white photography for the early days to the overcharged grease-pencil illustration of later years, stressing the inevitable "mediatization" of architectural activity. With the dramatic sense that pervades much of the work, cinematic devices replace conventional description. Architecture becomes the discourse of events as much as the discourse of spaces.

From our work in the early days, when event, movement, and spaces were analytically juxtaposed in mutual tension, the work moved toward an increasingly synthetic attitude. We had begun with a critique of the city, had gone back to basics: to simple and pure spaces, to barren landscapes, a room; to simple body movements, walking in a straight line, dancing; to short scenarios. And we gradually increased the complexity by introducing literary parallels and sequences of events, placing these programs within existing urban contexts. Within the worldwide megalopolis, new programs are placed in new urban situations. The process has gone full circle: it started by deconstructing the city, today it explores new codes of *assemblage.*

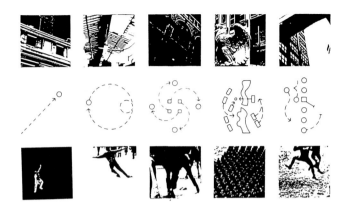

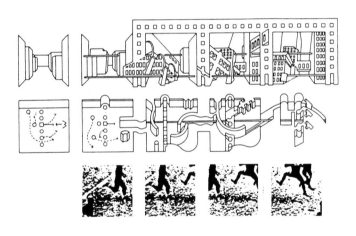

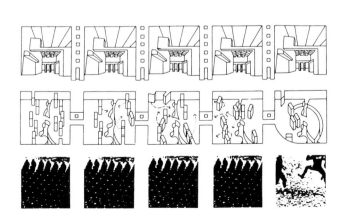

Bernard Tschumi, "Part 4: The Block," from *The Manhattan Transcripts*.

Bernard Tschumi, *Screenplays* (The Fight), 1977.

Bernard Tschumi, *Screenplays* (Psycho Dissolve), 1977.

Bernard Tschumi, *Screenplays* (Domino Distortion), 1979.

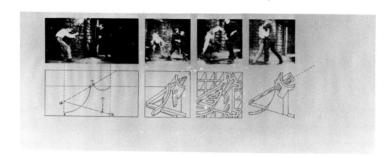

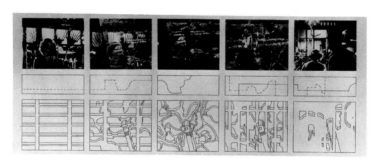

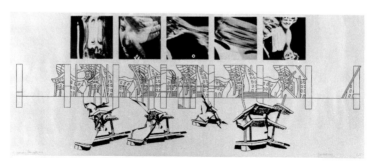

Sequences

———

Any architectural sequence includes or implies at least three relations. First, an internal relation, which deals with the method of work; then two external relations—one dealing with the juxtaposition of actual spaces, the other with program (occurrences or events). The first relation, or *transformational* sequence, can also be described as a device, a procedure. The second *spatial* sequence is constant throughout history; its typological precedents abound and its morphological variations are endless. Social and symbolic connotations characterize the third relation; we shall call it for now the *programmatic* sequence.[1]

One customary mode of architectural drawing already implies a transformational sequence. Successive layers of transparent tracing paper are laid one upon another, each with its respective variations, around a basic theme or *parti.* Each subsequent reworking leads to or refines the organizing principle. The process is generally based on intuition, precedents, and habit.

This sequence can also be based on a precise, rational set of transformational rules and discrete architectural elements. The sequential transformation then becomes its own theoretical object, insofar as the process becomes the result, while the sum of transformations counts at least as much as the outcome of the final transformation.

Transformational sequences tend to rely on the use of *devices,* or rules of transformation, such as compression, rotation, insertion, and transference. They can also display particular sets of variations, multiplications, fusions, repetitions, inversions, substitutions, metamorphoses, anamorphoses, dissolutions. These devices can be applied to the transformation of spaces as well as programs.

There are closed sequences of transformation as well as open ones. Closed sequences have a predictable end because the chosen rules ultimately imply the exhaustion of a process, its circularity, or its repetition. The open ones are sequences without closures, where new elements of transformation can be added at will according to other criteria, such as concurrent or juxtaposed sequences of another order—say, a narrative or programmatic structure, juxtaposed to the formal transformational structure.

Roland Barthes, in the "Structural Analysis of Narratives," defining a sequence: "A logical succession of nuclei bound together by a relation of solidarity: the sequence opens when one of its terms has no solitary antecedent and closes when another of its terms has no consequences."[2]

Sequences of space, *configurations-en-suite, enfilades,* spaces aligned along a common axis—all are specific architectural organizations, from Egyptian temples through the churches of the quattrocento to the present. All have emphasized a planned path with fixed halting points, a family of spatial points linked by continuous movement.

Sequences of transformation and sequences of spaces rarely intersect, as if architects carefully distinguished means of inception from end product through a sort of discrete restraint that does not reveal the maker's artifices in the final result and favors the certainty of a well-defined axis over the passionate uncertainties of thought.

If spatial sequences can be obviously manifest differences of geometrical *form* (the Villa Adriana), they can also differ by *dimension* alone, while maintaining similar geometrical form (the Ducal Palace at Urbino). They can even steadily increase in complexity, be constructed, step-by-step—or deconstructed—according to any rule or device.

Spatial transformations can be included within the time sequence—for example, through continuous scenery such as Frederick Kiesler's 1923 space stage set for Eugene O'Neill's *Emperor Jones.*

Luigi Moretti, writing on the spatial sequences and abstract relationships of Palladio's Palazzo Thiene in Vicenza: "In their pure dimensions, the sequences can be equated graphically as circles whose radii are proportional to the sphere corresponding in volume to each surrounding and whose center coincides with the center of gravity of the volume itself and is marked at the distance which in proportion this center has from the base plane of the spaces, that is from the level of the plinth."[3]

Spatial sequences can also display mixed formal devices. Moretti, again, writing on Palladio's Villa Rotunda: "in the density of light, the volumes go from portico to hall in the order of maximum to minimum, while in dimensions, the order is medium, least, greatest."

Yet architecture is inhabited: sequences of events, use, activities, incidents are always superimposed on those fixed spatial sequences. These are the programmatic sequences that suggest secret maps and impossible fictions, rambling collections of events all strung along a collection of spaces, frame after frame, room after room, episode after episode.

Is there ever a causal link between a formal system of spaces and a system of events? Rimbaud wondered whether vowels possessed colors, whether the letter *a* was red or blue. Similarly, do cylindrical spaces go with religion and rectangular ones with industry? Is there ever a homology between systems, a one-to-one relationship between space and event, between form and function, two systems that evoke and attract one another?

Adding events to the autonomous spatial sequence is a form of *motivation,* in the sense the Russian formalists gave to motivation, that is, whereby the "procedure" and its devices are the *raison d'être* of literature, and "content" is a simple *a posteriori* justification of form.

Alternately, is adding space to the autonomous sequence of events a reverse form of motivation? Or is it merely an extended form of *programmation*? Any predetermined sequence of events can always be turned into a program.

Program: "a descriptive notice, issued beforehand, of any formal series of proceedings, as a festive celebration, a course

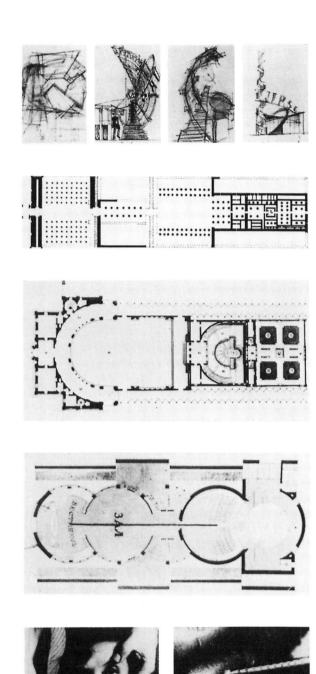

Konstantin Melnikov, preliminary sketches for the Soviet Pavilion, Paris Exhibition, 1924.

Floor plan of Temple, Karnak, Egypt. Reconstructed by Pococke. Reprinted by Quatremère de Quincy, 1803.

Vignola and Ammanti, floor plan for Villa Guilia, Rome, 1952.

Konstantin Melnikov, floor plan for *Worker's Club*, Moscow, 1929.

Luis Bunuel and Salvador Dali, *Un Chien Andalou*, 1928.

of study, etc. . . . , a list of the items or 'numbers' of a concert, etc., in the order of performance; hence the items themselves collectively, the performance as a whole. . . ."[4]

Programs fall into three categories: those that are indifferent to the spatial sequence, those that reinforce it, and those that work obliquely or against it.

Indifference: sequences of events and sequences of spaces can be largely independent of one another—say, assortments of exotic stalls among the regular columniation of the 1851 Crystal Palace. One then observes a strategy of indifference in which formal considerations do not depend on utilitarian ones. (The battalion marches on the fields.)

Reciprocity: Sequences of spaces and sequences of events can, of course, become totally interdependent and fully condition each other's existence—say *"machines à habiter,"* ideal Werkbund kitchens, space-age vessels where each action, each movement is designed, *programmed*. One then observes a strategy of reciprocity in which each sequence actually reinforces the other—the sort of architectural tautology favored by functionalist doctrines. (The skater skates on the skating rink.)

Conflict: sequences of events and spaces occasionally clash and contradict each other. One then observes a strategy of conflict in which each sequence constantly transgresses the other's internal logic. (The battalion skates on the tightrope.)

In themselves, spatial sequences are independent of what happens in them. (Yesterday I cooked in the bathroom and slept in the kitchen.) They may coincide for a shorter or longer period. As sequences of events do not depend on spatial sequences (and vice versa), both can form independent systems, with their own implicit schemes of parts.

Spatial sequences are generally structural; that is, they can be viewed or experienced independently of the meaning they may occasionally evoke. Programmatic sequences are generally inferential; conclusions or inferences can be drawn from the events or the "decor" that provide the sequence's connotative aspects. Such opposition is, of course, quite artificial; these distinctions do not exist separately.

Events "take place." And again. And again.

The linearity of sequences orders events, movements, spaces into a single progression that either combines or parallels divergent concerns. It provides "security" and at least one overriding rule against architectural fears.

Not all architecture is linear, nor is it all made of spatial additions, of detachable parts and clearly defined entities. Circular buildings, grid cities, *as well as* accumulations of fragmentary perspectives and cities without beginnings or ends, produce scrambled structures where meaning is derived from the order of experience rather than the order of composition.

Mies van der Rohe's Barcelona Pavilion: dissociation, fragmentation of unitary space. There is one sequence of direct vision and one for the experience of the body where a set of indeterminate and equivocal articulations suggests a multiplicity of readings. Its spatial sequence is nevertheless organized around a *thematic* structure, a series of variations around a limited number of elements that play the role of the fundamental theme—the *paradigm.*

By order of experience, one speaks of time, of chronology, of repetition. But some architects are suspicious of time and would wish their buildings to be read at a glance, like billboards.

Sequences have emotional value. Moretti, again, discussing St. Peter's: "pressure (access doors), limited liberation (atrium), opposition (atrium walls), very short pressure (basilica doors), total liberation (transversal of nave), final contemplation (space of central system)."

Like snapshots at key moments in the making of architecture, whether in the procedure or real space. Like a series of frozen frames.

If the spatial sequence inevitably implies the movement of an observer, then such movement can be objectively mapped and formalized—sequentially. Movement notation: an extension from the drawn conventions of choreography, it attempts to eliminate the preconceived meanings given to particular actions in order to concentrate on their spatial effects: the movement of bodies in space (dancers, footballers, acrobats).

For Lautréamont, to move is never to go from one place to the next, but always to execute some figure, to assume a certain body rhythm. "He is running away . . . he is running away." Or "the mad woman who passes by, dancing."

S	E	M
Space	Event	Movement

The final meaning of any sequence is dependent on the relation space/event/movement. By extension, the meaning of any architectural situation depends on the relation S E M.

The composite sequence SEM breaks the linearity of the elementary sequence, whether S, E, or M.

———

But architectural sequences do not mean only the reality of actual buildings, or the symbolic reality of their fictions. An implied narrative is always there, whether of method, use, or form. It combines the presentation of an event (or chain of events) with its progressive spatial interpretation (which of course alters it). Such, for instance, are *rituals* and their routes of initiation where, from points of entry to point of arrival, successive challenges await the new candidate. Here, the order of the sequence is intrinsic. The route is more important than any one place along it.

———

A ritual implies a near-frozen relationship between space and event. It institutes a new order against the disorder it aims to avoid. When it becomes necessary to mediate the tension between events and spaces and fix it by custom, then no single fragment must escape attention. Nothing strange or unexpected must happen. Control must be absolute.

———

Partial control is exercised through the use of the frame. Each frame, each part of a sequence qualifies, reinforces, or alters the parts that precede and follow it. The associations so formed allow for a plurality of interpretations rather than a singular fact. Each part is thus both complete and incomplete. And each part is a statement against indeterminacy; indeterminacy is always present in the sequence, irrespective of its methodological, spatial, or narrative nature.

———

Gap / closure / gap / closure / gap / closure

———

Is there such a thing as an architectural narrative? A narrative not only presupposes a sequence but also a language. As we all know, the "language" of architecture, the architecture "that speaks," is a controversial matter. Another question: If such architectural narrative corresponds to the narrative of literature, would space intersect with signs to give us a *discourse*?

———

The ability to translate narrative from one medium to another—to translate *Don Juan* into a play, an opera, a ballet, a film or comic strip—suggests architectural equivalences, equivalences that are not made by analogy to an architectural strip of course, but through carefully observed parallels. Terragni's *Danteum* does not tell us a story of events but reminds us about the temporality of a search—the impossibility of being at several places at the same time—a special type of allegory wherein every element initially corresponds to a physical reality.

———

The use of a plot may suggest the sense of an ending, an end to the overall organization. It superimposes a conclusion to the open-endedness of the transformational (or methodological) sequence. Whenever a program or "plot" (the single-family house, or "Cinderella") is well known (as are most architectural programs), only the "retelling" counts: the "telling" has been done enough.

———

Sequence (after J.-L. Godard): "Surely you agree, Mr. Architect, that buildings should have a base, a middle, and a top?" "Yes, but not necessarily in that order."

In literature and in the cinema, sequences can be manipulated by such devices as flashbacks, crosscuttings, close-ups, and dissolves. Are the inclusions of baroque details in the modern architectural sequence . . . temporary flashbacks?

Forms of composition: collage sequences (collisions) or montage sequences (progressions).

Contracted sequences fragment individual spaces and actions into discrete segments. In this manner, we might see the beginning of a use in space followed immediately by the beginning of another in a further space. Contracted sequences have occasionally reduced architecture's three dimensions into one (Le Corbusier's Villa Stein at Garches). The *expanded* sequence makes a solid of the gap between spaces. The gap thus becomes a space of its own, a corridor, threshold, or doorstep—a proper symbol inserted between each event (John Hejduk's Wall House). Combinations of expanded and contracted sequences can form special series, either coordinated or rhythmical.

All sequences are cumulative. Their "frames" derive significance from juxtaposition. They establish memory—of the preceding frame, of the course of events. To experience and to follow an architectural sequence is to reflect upon events in order to place them into successive wholes. The simplest sequence is always more than a *configuration-en-suite,* even if there is no need to specify the nature of each episode.

———

Frame: the moments of the sequence. Examining architecture "frame by frame," as through a film-editing machine.

———

Frames are both the *framing device*—conforming, regular, solid—and the *framed material*—questioning, distorting, and displacing. Occasionally the framing device can itself become the object of distortions and the framed material be conformist and orderly.

———

The frame permits the extreme formal manipulations of the sequence, for the content of congenial frames can be mixed, superimposed, dissolved, or cut up, giving endless possibilities to the narrative sequence. At the limit, these material manipulations can be classified according to formal strategies such as repetition, disjunction, distortion, dissolution, or insertion. For example, devices such as the insertion of additional elements within the sequence can change the meaning of the sequence as well as its impact on the experiencing subject, as in the well-known Kuleshov experiment, where the same shot of the actor's impassive face is introduced in a variety of situations, and the audience reads different expressions in each successive juxtaposition.

———

Parameters that remain constant and passive for the duration of the sequence can be added and transferred, as when a given

Courtyard in Amsterdam, c. seventeenth century.

Nathan Altman, *Re-enactment of the Revolution,* Design for Palace Square, Petrograd 1918.

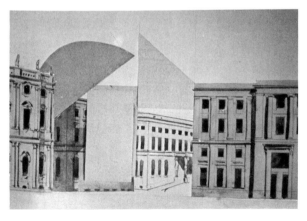

spatial configuration (the "circle") repeatedly passes from frame to frame, from room to room: a *displacement*.

___

All transformational devices (repetition, distortion, etc.) can apply equally and independently to spaces, events, or movements. Thus we can have a repetitive sequence of spaces (the successive courtyards of a Berlin block) coupled with an additive sequence of events (dancing in the first court, fighting in the second, skating in the third).

___

Alternatively, of course, architectural sequences can also be made strategically disjunctive (the pole-vaulter in the catacombs).

III Disjunction | essays written between 1984 and 1991

Bernard Tschumi, Parc de la Villette: Programmatic deconstruction: the largest common denominator = the *folie*.

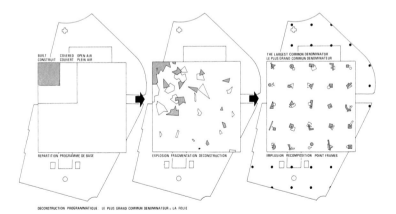

DECONSTRUCTION PROGRAMMATIQUE   LE PLUS GRAND COMMUN DENOMINATEUR = LA FOLIE

Madness and the Combinative ▬

The following essay consists of two distinct texts. The first deals with concepts of madness and transference; the second with ideas of combination and contamination. Both texts relate to one another in the same way that science relates to technique, that interpretation relates to fact—as an uncomfortable necessity.

1. Madness

> Madness would then be a word in perpetual discordance with itself
> and interrogative throughout, so that it would question its own
> possibility, and therefore the possibility of the language that would
> contain it; thus it would question itself, since the latter also belongs
> to the game of language.
>
> Maurice Blanchot

Madness serves as a constant point of reference throughout
the Urban Park of La Villette because it appears to illustrate
a characteristic situation at the end of the twentieth century—that of disjunctions and dissociations between use,
form, and social values. This situation is not necessarily a
negative one, but rather is symptomatic of a new condition,
as distant from eighteenth-century humanism as from this
century's various modernisms. Madness, here, is linked to
its psychoanalytical meaning—insanity—and can be related
to its built sense—folly—only with extreme caution.[1] The
aim is to free the built *folie* from its historical connotations
and to place it on a broader and more abstract plane, as an
autonomous object that, in the future, will be able to receive
new meanings.

The following text attempts to place architecture in general, and La Villette in particular, within a
specific methodological context, drawing on another theoretical field—namely, psychoanalysis. This contamination

of one discipline by another should also be read as a symptom of today's dislocated condition.

It is not necessary to recall in this context how Michel Foucault, in *Madness and Civilization*, analyzes the manner in which insanity raises questions of a sociological, philosophical, and psychoanalytic nature. If I suggest that madness also raises an architectural question, it is in order to demonstrate two points. On one hand, that normality ("good" architecture: typologies, modern movement dogmas, rationalism, and the other "isms" of recent history) is only one possibility among those offered by the combination or "genetics" of architectural elements. On the other, that, just as all collectivities require lunatics, deviants, and criminals to mark their own negativity, so architecture needs extremes and interdictions to inscribe the reality of its constant oscillation between the pragmatics of the built realm and the absoluteness of concepts. There is no intention here to descend into an intellectual fascination with madness, but rather to stress that madness articulates something that is often negated in order to preserve a fragile cultural or social order.

One of Jacques Lacan's contributions, on a methodological level, has been to suggest a psychoanalytical theory that, while informed by clinical practice, could not be reduced to that practice. The same concern exists today in architecture, whereby architectural theory is informed by what exists—space, the body, movement, history—but cannot, under any circumstances, be reduced to such factors alone. First *The Manhattan Transcripts* and then the *Folies* aimed at developing a related theory that would take into account both the unexpected and the aleatory, the pragmatic and the passionate, and would turn into reason what was formerly excluded from the realm of architecture because it seemed to belong to the realm of the irrational.

Dissociation, Transference, Anchoring Point   It is unnecessary to state again the disjunctions characterizing our time, as opposed to the false certainties generally propagated by architectural ideologists. The noncoincidence between being and meaning, man and object have been explored from Nietzsche to Foucault, from Joyce to Lacan. Who, then, could claim, today, the ability to recognize objects and people as part of a homogeneous and coherent world?

Much of the practice of architecture—composition, the ordering of objects as a reflection of the order of the world, the perfection of objects, the vision of a future made of progress and continuity—is conceptually inapplicable today. For architecture only exists through the world in which it locates itself. If this world implies dissociation and destroys unity, architecture will inevitably reflect these phenomena. The excesses of style—Doric supermarkets, Bauhaus bars, and Gothic condos—have emptied the language of architecture of meaning. The excess of meaning lacks meaning. But how can meaning be produced when signs only refer to other signs; when they do not signify, but only substitute? "A sign is not a sign of something, but of an effect which is what assumes as such the functioning of the signifier," notes Lacan; "Smoke is nothing but the sign of the smoker."[2]

But if signs are variables that are regularly displaced, there are other constants, such as form. In architecture, as elsewhere, the meaning of form resides only in the fact that form can be identified, and no more: "Form does not know more than it expresses. It is real, inasmuch as it contains being. Form is the knowledge of being."[3] Grasping fragments of life is linked to the identification of forms in space.

When confronted with the dispersion, the depersonalization, the dispossession of contemporary architecture, the analogy with psychoanalysis is possible and even correct. Numerous works on schizophrenia have shown how the schizophrenic hides in another mode of being in order to exist, existing outside the body and losing origins, protective limits, identity, and part of personal history. "In schizophrenia, something takes place that fully disturbs the relation of the subject to reality and drowns content with form."[4] Indeed, the schizophrenic places words and things on the same plane without distinguishing their respective origins.

In this analogy, the contemporary city and its many parts (here La Villette) are made to correspond with the dissociated elements of schizophrenia. The question becomes that of knowing one's relationship to such dislocated city parts. My hypothesis, here, is that this relationship necessarily suggests the idea of the transference. The transference in architecture resembles the psychoanalytic situation, the tool through which theoretical reconstruction of the totality of the subject is attempted. "Transference is taken here as transport: dissociation explodes transference into fragments of transference."[5] In the La Villette project, one speaks of a "formalization," an acting-out of dissociation. In a psychoanalytical situation, the transference fragments are transported to the psychotherapist. In an architectural situation, these transference fragments can only be transported onto architecture itself. The approach behind La Villette suggests meeting points, anchoring points where fragments of dislocated reality can be apprehended.

In this situation, the formation of the dissociation requires that a support be structured as a point of reassembly. The point of the *folie* becomes the focus of this dissociated space; it acts as a common denominator, constituting itself as a system of relations between objects, events, and people. It allows the development of a charge, a point of intensity.[6]

The grid of *folies* permits the combination of places of transference on the background of the La Villette site. Obviously, it is secondary to try to determine in advance the architectural forms that are most appropriate to such transferential situations. All that counts is that the *folie* is both the place and the object of transference. This fragmentary transference in madness is nothing but the production of an ephemeral regrouping of exploded or dissociated structures.

The psychoanalytical analogy ends here. Indeed, in the patient's world, a new factor would intervene, the symbolic factor, which for the psychoanalyst is one of the constituting factors of reality. However, the anchoring point—the *folie*—keeps a synthesizing function. It plays the role of the analyst; it allows a passage from rupture (a spatial notion) to conflict (a temporal notion). The anchoring point—*folie*—permits a multidimensional approach, reinforcing the transference fragments and introducing a restructuring on new bases (once deconstructed, reality can never be reconstructed as before).

These points of reference are organized in the form of a point grid. Such a structure inherently suggests the bars of the asylum or prison, introducing a diagram of order in the disorder of reality. In this manner the *folie* serves as a "securing" presence within a new reference system.

The point grid is a strategic tool of the La Villette project. It both articulates space and activates it. While refusing all hierarchies and "compositions," it plays a political role, rejecting the ideological a priori of the masterplans of the past. The Urban Park at La Villette offers the possibility of a restructuring of a dissociated world through an intermediary space—*folies*—in which the grafts of transference can take hold.

The point grid of *folies* constitutes the place of a new investment. The *folies* are new markings: the grafts of transference. These transference grafts allow access to space: one begins with an ambivalence toward a form in space that must be "reincarnated." The *folies* create a "nodal point where symbol and reality permit the building of the imaginary by reintroducing a dialectic of space and time."[7]

The park at La Villette offers such a transition space, a form of access to new cultural and social forms in which expression is possible, even when speech has disappeared.

La Villette, then, can be seen as an innovative exposition of a technique on the level of superimpositions and anchoring points. It offers places to apprehend objects and uses. It "builds itself into a mechanism that acts as reassembling unit for all the modes of locating."[8] It is a surface of multireferential anchoring points for things or people that leads to a partial coherence, yet challenges the institutional structure of official culture, urban parks, museums, leisure centers, and so on.

2. Combination

Although every creation is of necessity combinative, society, by virtue of the old romantic myth of 'inspiration' cannot stand being told so.

Roland Barthes, *Sade, Fourier, Loyola*

The fragmentation of our contemporary "mad" condition inevitably suggests new and unforeseen regroupings of its fragments. No longer linked in a coherent whole, independent from their past, these autonomous fragments can be recombined through a series of permutations whose rules have nothing to do with those of classicism or modernism.

The following pages attempt to demonstrate, first, that any "new" architecture implies the idea of combination, that all form is the result of a combination. It then proceeds to indicate that the notion of combination can be articulated into different categories. It should be emphasized that architecture is not seen here as the result of composition, a synthesis of formal concerns and functional constraints, but rather as part of a complex process of transformational relations. Between *pure formalism*, which reduces architecture to a series of forms (which at the limit, could be "formless" and meaningless), and *classical realism*, which attempts to give all forms an expressive value, aspects of *structural analysis* (which concerns us here) attempt to distinguish the nature of such transformational relations.

The purpose of this discussion is not to propose the kind of new moral or philosophical role often associated with architectural endeavors. Instead, it aims to consider the architect first as a formulator, an inventor of relations. It also aims to analyze what will be called in this context the *"combinative,"* that is, the set of combinations and permutations that is possible among different categories of analysis (space, movement, event, technique, symbol, etc.), as opposed to the more traditional play between function or use and form or style.

In this perspective, architecture is regarded as no longer concerned with composition or with the expression of function. Instead, it is seen as the object of permutation, the combination of a large set of variables, which is meant to relate, either in a manifest or secret way, domains as different as the act of running, double expansion joints, and the free plan. Such a play of permutations is not gratuitous. It permits new and hitherto unimagined activities to occur. However, it also implies that any attempt to find a new model or form of architecture requires an analysis of the full range of possibilities, as in the permutational matrices used by research scientists and structuralists alike. Indeed, perhaps the most important legacy of structuralism has to do with heuristics, demonstrating that meaning is always a function of both position and surface, produced by the movement of an empty slot in the series of a structure.

The guiding principle of research on La Villette is precisely that of the empty slot. This play of permutations was initially explored in *The Manhattan Transcripts;* "the football player skates on the battlefield"[9] was the manifesto of the interchangeability of objects, people, and events. Influenced by poststructuralist texts as much as by the different techniques of film montage, the *Transcripts* were only introducing, in a theoretical manner, what is to be applied at La Villette.

Obviously, combination techniques are not without precedent. Sadian practice, as analyzed by Barthes in *Sade, Fourier, Loyola,* gives a clear example: In Sade, all functions are interchangeable; there are only classes of actions as opposed to groups of individuals. The subject of an action can be turned into its object; it can also be a libertine, a victim, a helper, a spouse. The erotic code takes advantage of the logic of language and its varied permutations. Sade demonstrates: "in order to combine incest, adultery, sodomy, and sacrilege, he buggers his married daughter with a host."[10] Within the same system Sade juxtaposes heterogeneous fragments belonging to different domains, generally segregated by social taboos ("the Pope's ass"). What is unlikely on the initial level, that is, "a turkey whipped by an armless dwarf," "a staircase perched on a tightrope," becomes both a possibility of discourse and a poetic device. Contamination touches all "styles" of discourse.

In a remarkable study entitled *Palimpsestes*,[11] the literary critic Gérard Genette has refined these concepts of transformation. Combination, he writes, exists only within a complex system of transformational relations. These relations can act on whole texts as much as on fragments. In the case that concerns us, that of La Villette, a general type of transformation called *"mechanical operations"* can be distinguished. Mechanical operations may take several forms: (a) that of "lexical" permutations, as in the decomposition of the 10m × 10m × 10m cube of the original *folie* into a series of discrete fragments or elements, that is, square or rectangular rooms, ramps, cylindrical stairs, and so forth, which have been ordered to form a catalogue or lexicon. A lexical permutation entails taking an element from the original cube and mechanically replacing it with another form from the lexicon (for example, e + 7: each element of the cube is exchanged for the element of the lexicon placed in seventh position behind it); or (b) that of "hypertextual" permutation, by which an element of the cube will be replaced by another—for example, by a nineteenth-century neoclassical pavilion placed nearby on the site. Such transplantation may lead to a semantic transformation in terms of its new context.

Disjunction

Bernard Tschumi, Dokumenta *Folies*. Kasel Town Hall deconstruction, 1980.

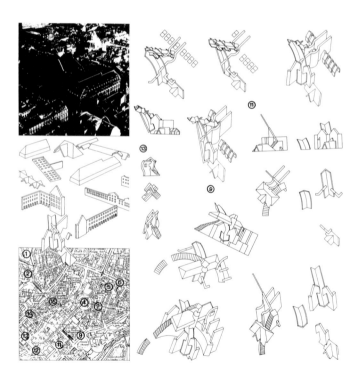

A series of transformations and permutations similar to the manipulations of the writers Raymond Queneau and Georges Perec derives from the notion of the mechanical operation. This mixing technique, generally known as "contamination," can take innumerable forms. It is characterized by the purely mechanical aspect of the transformation, thus distinguishing it from pastiche or parody, which carefully divert a text from its initial context toward a use with a meaning known well in advance. No semantic intention governs the transformations of La Villette; they result from the application of a device or formula. While this may superficially resemble a variation on the surrealist "exquisite corpse," we have seen earlier that the relation between form and meaning is never one between signifer and signified. Architectural relations are never semantic, syntactic, or formal, in the sense of formal logic. Instead, a better analogy to these montage and mixing techniques might be found in Dziga Vertov's or Sergei Eisenstein's work in the cinema, Queneau's in literature, or in the finite variations around an initial theme that one finds in J. S. Bach's *Fugues.*

However, were this process only to involve deriving transformations and permutations on the level of the solid elements of architecture, such as walls, stairs, windows, and moldings, it would not differ significantly from most research on modes of composition or transformation as such. In contrast, and in opposition to functionalist, formalist, classical, and modernist doctrines, my ambition, already expressed in *The Manhattan Transcripts,* is to deconstruct architectural norms in order to reconstruct architecture along different axes; to indicate that space, movement, and event are inevitably part of a minimal definition of architecture, and that the contemporary disjunction between use, form, and social values suggests an interchangeable relation between object, movement, and action. In this manner, the program becomes an integral part of architecture, and each element of this program becomes an element of permutation akin to solid elements.

No permutation is "innocent": just as the form of a text cannot be changed without altering its meaning, so no permutation of program, space, or movement fails to achieve a shift in meaning. The transformation alters events less than their meaning. Specifically, three basic types of relations can be distinguished: (a) the reciprocal relation, for example, to skate on the skating rink; (b) the indifferent relation, for example, to skate in the schoolyard; and (c) the conflictual relation, for example, to skate in the chapel, to skate on the tightrope. According to the strict terms of logic, nothing differentiates (a) from (c). However, the actual difference between the normative "a" and the disjunctive "c," that is, between a functional reciprocal relation and a conflictual relation, generally depends on a moral or aesthetic judgment, which is external to architecture and highly variable. Hence according to circumstances, a functional building can become conflictual or vice versa. The only distribution that counts, then, is one of motivation.

Similarly, all new relations emit "erotic" charges. Besides an obvious theoretical motivation, the invention of new relations ("the battalion skates on the tightrope") may correspond to an insistent need to force architecture to say more than it is capable of saying (if I skate on the battlefield, I bring about an erotic displacement.)[12]

La Villette In the La Villette project two alternative strategies to establish a basis for such combinative research emerged at the outset. The stated concern of the project was to apply theoretical concerns on a practical level, to move from the "pure mathematics" of *The Manhattan Transcripts* to applied mathematics. The first possible strategy was to employ specific "texts" or architectural precedents (Central Park, Tivoli, etc.) as starting points and adapt them (in the sense of a movie adaptation of a book), to the site and the program. This strategy implied considering a preexistent spatial organization as a "model" that could either be *adapted* or *transformed* in the manner that Joyce "transformed" Homer's *Odyssey*. This method had already been applied in Part I of *The Manhattan Transcripts* (The Park),[13] in which Central Park acts as the original or "hypotext" for the contemporary "hypertext" of the *Transcripts*. The other strategy involved ignoring built precedents so as to begin from a neutral mathematical configuration or ideal topological configurations (grids, linear or concentric systems, etc.) that could become the points of departure for future transformations. This second approach was the one selected: three autonomous abstract systems—systems of points, lines, and surfaces—were laid out. Independent, each with its own internal logic, these three systems would then begin to *contaminate* one another when superimposed.

A fundamental distinction separates these two strategies. In the first case, the design is the result of the transformations, while in the second it becomes the origin. Rather than the outcome of a thinking process, the design, in the latter instance, provides the starting point for a long series of transformations that slowly lead to the built reality. In this sense, it is a mutually implicating structure, both hypotext and hypertext.

Processes of combination, permutation, and transformation—or, more generally speaking, of derivation—can, of course, be classified within a large number of operative types. To apply or "expose" all within a single project would detract from the genuine architectural purpose: to permit new and hitherto unimagined situations and activities to occur. However, a brief delineation of some of the characteristic types of derivation, applicable as design tools or as instruments of critical analysis, seems necessary. The two main types of derivation are imitation and transformation. To quote Genette: "A copy is the paradoxical state of (maximal) imitative effect obtained by a (minimal) transformative effort."[14] Parody, pastiche, and "digest" do, of course, display different degrees of imitation and can be found in the varied neoclassical imitations of recent architectural history. Although imitation and transformation are antithetical, the extreme positive of one corresponding to the extreme negative of the other, they exist in varying proportions in any attempt to exaggerate or saturate existing styles. For example, transstylization is stylistic rewriting, modernization means Shakespeare with leather jackets, Bernini with cantilevers. More specifically, transformation includes translongation (quantitative transformation) which can be divided into reduction (such as suppression, excision, amputation, miniaturization) and augmentation (such as addition, extension, rhetorical amplification, collage insertion, scale adjustment, etc.). Substitution equals expression plus addition. Distortion retains all elements but alters their appearance (compression, elongation, and so forth). Contamination implies a progressive shift from one reality to another (vocabulary by Mallarmé, syntax by Proust; plan by Le Corbusier, walls and columns by Mies van der Rohe). Permutation requires discrete, individual transformation. An important category is that of disjunction, dissociation, rupture, dislocation, and cut-ups.

The reason this series of transformational relations has been outlined is simple: the analysis of our present condition as a dislocated one suggests the possibility of future regroupings, just as particles of matter in space will occasionally concentrate and form new points of intensity, so the fragments of the dislocation can be reassembled in new and unexpected relations. One mode of rearrangement has been indicated in the first part of this text: it takes its model from the idea of transference. A possible means of such regrouping belongs to the techniques or devices described here as transformational relations, including the combinative.

Parc de la Villette, point grids.

Abstract Mediation and Strategy

When confronted with an urbanistic program, an architect may either:

a. Design a masterly construction, an inspired architectural gesture (a composition)
b. Take what exists, fill in the gaps, complete the text, scribble in the margins (a complement)
c. Deconstruct what exists by critically analyzing the historical layers that preceded it, even adding other layers

derived from elsewhere—from other cities, other parks (a palimpsest)

d. Search for an intermediary—an abstract system to mediate between the site (as well as all given constraints) and some other concept, beyond city or program (a mediation)

During the Parc de la Villette competition, thought had been given to employing as a methodology either the palimpsest or the abstract mediation. The composition and complement were rejected outright, the one for its subscription to old architectural myths, the other for its limiting pragmatism. Yet the palimpsest (which had been explored in the 1976 *Screenplays*) was not pursued, for its inevitably figurative or representational components were incompatible with the complexity of the programmatic, technical, and political constraints that could be foreseen. Furthermore, the object of the competition was both to select a chief architect who would be in charge of the master plan as well as of construction of the park's key elements, and to suggest, coordinate, and supervise possible contributions by other artists, landscape designers, and architects. The numerous unknowns governing the general economic and ideological context suggested that much of the chief architect's role would depend on a strategy of substitution. It was clear that the elements of the program were interchangeable and that budgets and priorities could be altered, even reversed, at least over the course of one generation.

Hence the concern, reinforced by recent developments in philosophy, art, and literature, that the park propose a strong conceptual framework while simultaneously suggesting multiple combinations and substitutions. One part could replace another, or a building's program be revised, changing (to use an actual example) from restaurant to gardening center to arts workshop. In this manner, the park's identity could be maintained, while the circumstantial logics of state or institutional politics could pursue their own independent scenarios. Moreover, our objective was also to act upon a strategy of differences: if other designers were to intervene, their projects' difference from the *Folies* or divergence from the continuity of the cinematic promenade would become the condition of their contributions. The general circumstances of the project, then, were to find an organizing structure that could exist independent of use, a structure without center or hierarchy, a structure that would negate the simplistic assumption of a causal relationship between a program and the resulting architecture.

Recourse to the point grid as an organizing structure was hardly without precedent. The concept of an abstract mediation had been researched earlier in *Joyce's Garden* (1977), in which a literary text, *Finnegans Wake*, was used as the program for a project involving a dozen contributions by different students on a "real" site, London's Covent Garden. The intersections of an ordinance survey grid became the locations of each architectural intervention, thereby accommodating a heterogeneous selection of buildings through the regular spacing of points. Moreover (and perhaps more important), the point grid functioned as a mediator between two mutually exclusive systems of words and stones, between the literary program (James Joyce's book) and the architectural text. *Joyce's Garden* in no way attempted to reconcile the disparities resulting from the superimposition of one text on another; it avoided synthesis, encouraging, instead, the opposed and often conflicting logics of the different systems. Indeed, the abstraction of the grid as an organizing device suggested the disjunction between an architectural signifier and its programmatic signified, between space and the use that is made of it. The point grid became the tool of an approach that argued, against functionalist doctrines, that there is no cause-and-effect relationship between the two terms of program and architecture.

Beyond such personal precedents, the point grid was also one of the few modes of spatial organization that vigorously resisted the stamp of the individual author: its historical multiplicity made it a sign without origin, an image without "first image" or inaugurating mark. Nevertheless, the grid's serial repetitions and seeming anonymity made it a paradigmatic twentieth-century form. And just as it resisted the humanist claim to authorship, so it opposed the closure of ideal compositions and geometric dispositions. Through its regular and repetitive markings, the grid defined a potentially infinite field of points of intensity: an incomplete, infinite extension, lacking center or hierarchy.

The grid, then, presented the project team with a series of dynamic oppositions. We had to design a park: the grid was antinature. We had to fulfill a number of functions: the grid was antifunctional. We had to be realists: the grid was abstract. We had to respect the local context: the grid was anticontextual. We had to be sensitive to site boundaries: the grid was infinite. We had to take into account political and economic indetermination: the grid was determinate. We had to acknowledge garden precedents: the grid had no origin, it opened onto an endless recession into prior images and earlier signs.

Superimposition

It should be noted that the point grid of La Villette could just as well have taken the form of a random distribution of points throughout the site. Only for strategic, rather than conceptual, reasons was the regular point grid selected. It is also important to recall that the point grid of *Folies* (the "system of points") constitutes only one of the project's components; the "system of lines" and the "system of surfaces" are as fundamental as the "system of points."

Each represents a different and autonomous system (a text), whose superimposition on another makes impossible any "composition," maintaining differences and refusing ascendency of any privileged system or organizing element. Although each is determined by the architect as "subject," when one system is superimposed on another, the subject—the architect—is erased. While one could object that the same architect continues his controlling authority by staging the superimposition (and hence that the park remains the product of his individual intentions), the competition requirements provided a means to relativize the presence of such a masterminding subject by stipulating, as in any large-scale urban project, that other professionals intervene. Another layer, another system could then be interposed among the preceding three layers in the form of occasional constructions juxtaposed to several *Folies,* or of experimental gardens by different designers, inserted into the sequences of the cinematic promenade. Such juxtapositions would be successful only insofar as they injected discordant notes into the system, hence reinforcing a specific aspect of the Park theory. The principle of heterogeneity—of multiple, dissociated, and inherently confrontational elements—is aimed at disrupting the smooth coherence and reassuring stability of composition, promoting instability and programmatic madness ("a Folie"). Other existing constructions (e.g., the Museum of Science and Industry, the Grande Halle) add further to the calculated discontinuity.

Cinegram

To the notion of composition, which implies a reading of urbanism on the basis of the *plan,* the La Villette project substitutes an idea comparable to montage (which presupposes autonomous parts or fragments). Film analogies are convenient, since the world of the cinema was the first to introduce discontinuity—a segmented world in which each fragment maintains its own independence, thereby permitting a multiplicity of combinations. In film, each frame (or photogram) is placed in continuous movement. Inscribing movement through the rapid succession of photograms constitutes the cinegram.

The Park is a series of cinegrams, each of which is based on a precise set of architectonic, spatial, or programmatic transformations. Contiguity and superimposition of cinegrams are two aspects of montage. Montage, as a technique, includes such other devices as repetition, inversion, substitution, and insertion. These devices suggest an art of rupture, whereby invention resides in contrast—even in contradiction.

Deconstruction

Is the Parc de la Villette a built theory or a theoretical building? Can the pragmatism of building practice be allied with the analytic rigor of concepts?

An earlier series of projects, published as *The Manhattan Transcripts*, was aimed at achieving a displacement of conventional architectural categories through a theoretical argument. La Villette was the built extension of a comparable method; it was impelled by the desire to move "from pure mathematics to applied mathematics." In its case, the constraints of the built realization both expanded and restricted the research. They expanded it, insofar as the very real economic, political, and technical constraints of the operation demanded an ever increasing sharpening of the theoretical argumentation: the project became better as difficulties increased. But they restricted it insofar as La Villette had to be *built:* the intention was never merely to publish books or mount exhibitions; the finality of each drawing was building: except in the book entitled *La Case Vide*, there were no theoretical drawings for La Villette.

However, the Parc de la Villette project had a specific aim: to prove that it was possible to construct a complex architectural organization without resorting to traditional rules of composition, hierarchy, and order. The principle of superimposition of three autonomous systems of points, lines, and surfaces was developed by rejecting the totalizing synthesis of objective constraints evident in the majority of large-scale projects. In fact, if historically architecture has always been defined as the "harmonious synthesis" of cost, structure, use, and formal constraints (*venustas, firmitas, utilitas*), the Park became architecture against itself: a dis-integration.

Our aims were to displace the traditional opposition between program and architecture, and to extend questioning of other architectural conventions through operations of superimposition, permutation, and substitution to achieve "a reversal of the classical oppositions and a general displacement of the system," as Jacques Derrida has written, in another context, in *Marges*.

Above all, the project directed an attack against cause-and-effect relationships, whether between form and function, structure and economics, or (of course) form and program, replacing these oppositions by new concepts of contiguity and superimposition. "Deconstructing" a given program meant showing that the program could challenge the very ideology it implied. And deconstructing architecture involved dismantling its conventions, using concepts derived both from architecture and from elsewhere—from cinema, literary criticism, and other disciplines. For if the limits between different domains of thought have gradually vanished in the past twenty years, the same phenomenon applies to architecture, which now entertains relations with cinema, philosophy, and psychoanalysis (to cite only a few examples) in an intertextuality subversive of modernist autonomy. But it is above all the historical split between architecture and its theory that is eroded by the principles of deconstruction.

It is not by chance that the different systems of the Park negate one another as they are superimposed on the site. Much of my earlier theoretical work had questioned the very idea of structure, paralleling contemporary research on literary texts. One of the goals at La Villette was to pursue this investigation of the concept of structure, as expressed in the respective forms of the point grid, the coordinate axes (covered galleries) and the "random curve" (cinematic promenade). Superimposing these autonomous and completely logical structures meant questioning their conceptual status as ordering machines: the superimposition of three coherent structures can never result in a supercoherent megastructure, but in something undecidable, something that is the opposite of a totality. This device has been explored from

1976 onward in *The Manhattan Transcripts,* where the overlapping of abstract and figurative elements (based on "abstract" architectonic transformations as much as on "figurative" extracts from the selected site) coincided with a more general exploration of the ideas of program, scenario, and sequence.

The independence of the three superposed structures thus avoided all attempts to homogenize the Park into a totality. It eliminated the presumption of a preestablished causality between program, architecture, and signification. Moreover, the Park rejected context, encouraging intertextuality and the dispersion of meaning. It subverted context: La Villlette is anticontextual. It has no relation to its surroundings. Its plan subverts the very notion of borders on which "context" depends.

Non-sense/No-meaning

The Parc de la Villette project thus can be seen to encourage conflict over synthesis, fragmentation over unity, madness and play over careful management. It subverts a number of ideals that were sacrosanct to the modern period and, in this manner, it can be allied to a specific vision of postmodernity. But the project takes issue with a particular premise of architecture—namely, its obsession with presence, with the idea of a meaning immanent in architectural structures and forms that directs its signifying capacity. The latest resurgence of this myth has been the recuperation, by architects, of meaning, symbol, coding, and "double-coding," in an eclectic movement reminiscent of the long tradition of "revivalisms" and "symbolisms" appearing throughout history. The architectural postmodernism contravenes the reading evident in other domains, where postmodernism involves an assault on meaning or, more precisely, a rejection of a well-defined signified that guarantees the authenticity of the work of art. To dismantle meaning, showing that it is never transparent, but socially produced, was a key objective in a new critical approach that questioned the humanist assumptions of style. Instead, architectural postmodernism opposed the style of the modern movement, offering as an alternative another, more palatable style. Its nostalgic pursuit of coherence, which ignores today's social, political, and cultural dissociations, is frequently the avatar of a particularly conservative architectural milieu.

The La Villette project, in contrast, attempts to dislocate and deregulate meaning, rejecting the symbolic repertory of architecture as a refuge of humanist thought. For today the term *park* (like *architecture, science,* or *literature*) has lost its universal meaning; it no longer refers to a fixed absolute nor to an ideal. Not the *hortus conclusus* and not the replica of Nature, La Villette is a term in constant production, in continuous change; its meaning is never fixed but is always deferred, differed, rendered irresolute by the multiplicity of meanings it inscribes. The project aims to unsettle both memory and context, opposing many contextualist and continualist ideals that imply that the architect's intervention necessarily refers to a typology, origin, or determining signified. Indeed, the Park's architecture refuses to operate as the expression of a preexisting content, whether

Disjunction

Parc de la Villette, superpositions.

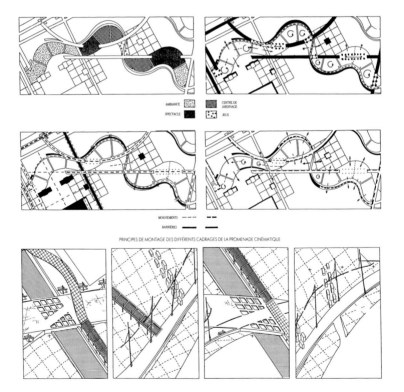

AMBIANCE SPECTACLE CENTRE DE JARDINAGE JEUX

MOUVEMENTS BARRIÈRES

PRINCIPES DE MONTAGE DES DIFFÉRENTS CADRAGES DE LA PROMENADE CINÉMATIQUE

subjective, formal, or functional. Just as it does not answer to the demands of the self (the sovereign or "creative" architect), so it negates the immanent dialectic of the form, since the latter is displaced by superimpositions and transformations of elements that always exceed any given formal configuration. Presence is postponed and closure deferred as each permutation or combination of form shifts the image one step ahead. Most important, the Park calls into question the fundamental or primary signified of architecture—its tendency (as Derrida remarks in *La Case Vide*) to be "in service, and at service," obeying an economy of meaning premised on functional use. In contrast, La Villette promotes programmatic instability, functional *Folie*. Not a plenitude, but instead "empty" form: *les cases sont vides*.

La Villette, then, aims at an architecture that *means nothing*, an architecture of the signifier rather than the signified—one that is pure trace or play of language. In a Nietzschean manner, La Villette moves toward interpretive infinity, for the effect of refusing fixity is not insignificance but semantic plurality. The Park's three autonomous and superimposed systems and the endless combinatory possibilities of the *Folies* give way to a multiplicity of impressions. Each observer will project his own interpretation, resulting in an account that will again be interpreted (according to psychanalytic, sociological, or other methodologies) and so on. In consequence, there is no absolute truth to the architectural project, for whatever meaning it may have is a function of interpretation: it is not resident in the object or in the object's materials. Hence, the truth of red *Folies* is not the truth of Constructivism, just as the truth of the system of points is not the truth of the system of lines. The addition of the systems' internal coherences is not coherent. The excess of rationality is not rational. La Villette looks out on new social and historical circumstances: a dispersed and differentiated reality that marks an end to the utopia of unity.

Program and Distanciation

At La Villette (or anywhere else, for that matter) there is no longer any relationship possible between architecture and program, architecture and meaning. It has been suggested, in discussing La Villette, that architecture must produce a distance between itself and the program it fulfills. This is comparable to the effect of distanciation first elaborated in the performing arts as the principle of nonidentity between actor and character. In the same way, it could be said that *there must be no identification* between architecture and program: a bank must not look like a bank, nor an opera house like an opera house, nor a park like a park. This distanciation can be produced either through calculated shifts in programmatic expectations or through the use of some mediating agent— an abstract parameter that acts as a distancing agent between the built realm and the user's demands (at La Villette, this agent was the grid of *Folies*).

The concept of program, however, remains increasingly important. By no means should it be eliminated (a "pure" architecture) or reinjected at the end of the development of a "pure" architectonic elaboration. The program plays the same role as narrative in other domains: it can and must be reinterpreted, rewritten, deconstructed by the architect. La Villette, in this sense, is dys-narrative or dys-programmatic: the programmatic content is filled with calculated distortions and interruptions, making for a city fragment in which each image, each event strives towards its very concept.

Of course, there are further ways to explore the impossible relation between architecture and program. The following examples are an indication of such a field of research.

Crossprogramming: Using a given spatial configuration for a program not intended for it, that is, using a church building for bowling. Similar to typological displacement: a town hall inside the spatial configuration of a prison or a museum inside a car park structure. Reference: crossdressing.

Transprogramming: Combining two programs, regardless of their incompatibilities, together with their respective spatial configurations. Reference: planetarium + rollercoaster.

Disprogramming: Combining two programs, whereby a required spatial configuration of program A contaminates program B and B's possible configuration. The new program B may be extracted from the inherent contradictions contained in program A, and B's required spatial configuration may be applied to A.

Bernard Tschumi, Exploded *Folie* 1984.

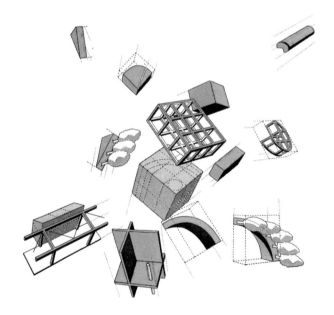

Disjunctions   ▬▬▬

1. Disjunction and Culture

The paradigm of the architect passed down to us through the modern period is that of the form-giver, the creator of hierarchical and symbolic structures characterized, on the one hand, by their unity of parts and, on the other, by the transparency of form to meaning. (The modern, rather than modernist, subject of architecture is referred to here so as to indicate that this unified perspective far exceeds our recent past.) A number of well-known correlatives elaborate these terms: the fusion of form and function, program and context, structure and meaning. Underlying these is a belief in the unified, centered, and self-generative subject, whose own autonomy is reflected in the formal autonomy of the work. Yet, at a certain point, this long-standing practice, which accentuates synthesis, harmony, the composition of elements and the seamless coincidence of potentially disparate parts, becomes estranged from its external culture, from contemporary cultural conditions.

2. Dis-structuring

In its disruptions and disjunctions, its characteristic fragmentation and dissociation, today's cultural circumstances suggest the need to discard established categories of meaning and contextual histories. It might be worthwhile, therefore, to abandon any notion of a postmodern architecture in favor of a "posthumanist" architecture, one that would stress not only the dispersion of the subject and the force of social regulation, but also the effect of such decentering on the entire notion of unified, coherent architectural form. It also seems important to think, not in terms of principles of formal composition, but rather of questioning structures—that is, the order, techniques, and procedures that are entailed by any architectural work.

Such a project is far removed from formalism in that it stresses the historical motivation of the sign, emphasizing its contingency, its cultural fragility, rather than a-historical essence. It is one that, in current times, can only confront the radical rift between signifier and signified or, in architectural terms, space and action, form and function. That today we are witnessing a striking dislocation of these terms calls attention not only to the disappearance of functionalist theories but perhaps also to the normative function of architecture itself.

3. Order

Any theoretical work, when "displaced" into the built realm, still retains its role within a general system or open system of thought. As in the theoretical project *The Manhattan Transcripts* (1981), and the built Parc de la Villette, what is questioned is the notion of unity. As they are conceived, both works have no beginnings and no ends. They are operations composed of repetitions, distortions, superpositions, and so forth. Although they have their own internal logic—they are not aimlessly pluralistic—their operations cannot be described purely in terms of internal or sequential transformations. The idea of order is constantly questioned, challenged, pushed to the edge.

4. Strategies of Disjunction

Although the notion of disjunction is not to be seen as an architectural concept, it has effects that are impressed upon the site, the building, even the program, according to the dissociative logic governing the work. If one were to define disjunction, moving beyond its dictionary meaning, one would insist on the idea of limit, of interruption. Both the *Transcripts* and La Villette employ different elements of a strategy of disjunction. This strategy takes the form of a systematic exploration of one or more themes: for example, frames and sequences in the case of the *Transcripts*, and superposition and repetition in La Villette. Such explorations can never be conducted in the abstract, *ex nihilo:* one works within the discipline of architecture—though with an awareness of other fields: literature, philosophy, or even film theory.

5. Limits

The notion of the limit is evident in the practice of Joyce, and Bataille and Artaud, who all worked at the edge of philosophy and nonphilosophy, of literature and nonliterature. The attention paid today to Jacques Derrida's deconstructive approach also represents an interest in the work at the limit: the analysis of concepts in the most rigorous and internalized manner, but also their analysis from without, so as to question what these concepts and their history hide, as repression or dissimulation. Such examples suggest that there is a need to consider the question of limits in architecture. They act as reminders (to me) that my own pleasure has never surfaced in looking at buildings, at the great works of the history or the present of architecture, but, rather, in dismantling them.

To paraphrase Orson Welles: "I don't like architecture, I like making architecture."

6. Notation

The work on notation undertaken in *The Manhattan Transcripts* was an attempt to deconstruct the components of architecture. The different modes of notation employed were aimed at grasping domains that, though normally excluded from most architectural theory, are indispensable to work at the margins, or limits, of architecture. Although no mode of notation, whether mathematical or logical, can transcribe the full complexity of the architectural phenomenon, the progress of architectural notation is linked to the renewal of both architecture and its accompanying concepts of culture. Once the traditional components have been dismantled, reassembly is an extended process; above all, what is ultimately a transgression of classical and modern canons should not be permitted to regress toward formal empiricism. Hence the disjunctive strategy used both in the *Transcripts* and at La Villette, in which facts never quite connect, and relations of conflict are carefully maintained, rejecting synthesis or totality. The project is never achieved, nor are the boundaries ever definite.

7. Disjunction and the Avant-garde

As Derrida points out, architectural and philosophical concepts do not disappear overnight. The once fashionable "epistemological break" notwithstanding, ruptures always occur within an old fabric that is constantly dismantled and dislocated in such a way that its ruptures lead to new concepts or structures. In architecture such disjunction implies that at no moment can any part become a synthesis or self-sufficient totality; each part leads to another, and every construction is off-balance, constituted by the traces of another construction. It could also be constituted by the traces of an event, a program. It can lead to new concepts, as one objective here is to understand a new concept of the city, of architecture.

If we were to qualify an architecture or an architectural method as "disjunctive," its common denominators might be the following:

- Rejection of the notion of "synthesis" in favor of the idea of dissociation, of disjunctive analysis
- Rejection of the traditional opposition between use and architectural form in favor of a superposition or juxtaposition of two terms that can be independently and similarly subjected to identical methods of architectural analysis
- Emphasis placed, as a method, on dissociation, superposition, and combination, which trigger dynamic forces that expand into the whole architectural system, exploding its limits while suggesting a new definition

The concept of disjunction is incompatible with a static, autonomous, structural view of architecture.

But it is not anti-autonomy or anti-structure; it simply implies constant, mechanical operations that systematically produce dissociation in space and time, where an architectural element only functions by colliding with a programatic element, with the movement of bodies, or whatever. In this manner, disjunction becomes a systematic and theoretical tool for the making of architecture.

Bernard Tschumi, Photogram, Proposal for Kansai Airport, 1989.

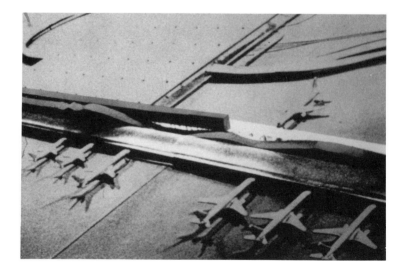

De-, Dis-, Ex-

━━━

Cities today have no visible limits. In America, they never had. In Europe, however, the concept of "city" once implied a closed and finite entity. The old city had walls and gates. But these have long ceased to function. Are there other types of gates, new gates to replace the gates of the past? Are the new gates those electronic warning systems installed in airports, screening passengers for weapons? Have electronics

Delivered as a lecture at the Dia Foundation in New York City in Fall 1987.

and, more generally, technology replaced the boundaries, the guarded borders of the past?

The walls surrounding the city have disappeared and, with them, the rules that made the distinction between inside and outside, despite politicians' and planners' guidelines, despite geographical and administrative boundaries. In *"L'Espace Critique"*, Paul Virilio develops a challenging argument for anyone concerned with the making of urban society: Cities have become *deregulated.* This deregulation is reinforced by the fact that much of the city does not belong to the realm of the visible anymore. What was once called urban design has been replaced by a composite of invisible systems. Why should architects still talk about monuments? Monuments are invisible now. They are *disproportionate*—so large (at the scale of the world) that they cannot be seen. Or so small (at the scale of computer chips) that they cannot be seen either.

Remember: architecture was first the art of measure, of proportions. It once allowed whole civilizations to measure time and space. But speed and the telecommunications of images have altered that old role of architecture. *Speed* expands time by contracting space; it negates the notion of physical dimension.

Of course, physical environment still exists. But, as Virilio suggests, the appearance of permanence (buildings as solid, made of steel, concrete, glass) is constantly challenged by the immaterial representation of abstract systems, from television to electronic surveillance, and so on. Architecture is constantly subject to reinterpretation. In no way can architecture today claim permanence of meaning. Churches are turned into movie houses, banks into yuppie restaurants, hat factories into artists' studios, subway tunnels into nightclubs, and sometimes nightclubs into churches. The supposed cause-and-effect relationship between function and form ("form follows function") is forever condemned the day function becomes almost as transient as those magazines and mass media images in which architecture now appears as such a fashionable object.

History, memory, and tradition, once called to the rescue by architectural ideologists, become nothing but modes of disguise, fake regulations, so as to avoid the question of transience and temporality.

When the philosopher Jean-François Lyotard speaks about the crisis of the grand narratives of modernity ("progress," the "liberation of humanity," etc.), it only prefigures the crisis of any narrative, any discourse, any mode of representation. The crisis of these grand narratives, their coherent totality, is also the crisis of limits. As with the contemporary city, there are no more boundaries delineating a coherent and homogeneous whole. On the contrary, we inhabit a fractured space, made of accidents, where figures are disintegrated, *dis*-integrated. From a sensibility developed during centuries around the "appearance of a stable image" ("balance," "equilibrium," "harmony"), today we favor a sensibility of the disappearance of unstable images: first movies (twenty-four images per second), then television, then computer-generated images, and recently (among a few architects) disjunctions, dislocations, deconstructions.

Virilio argues that the abolition of permanence—through the collapse of the notion of distance as a time factor—confuses reality. First deregulation of airlines, then deregulation of Wall Street, finally deregulation of appearances: it all belongs to the same inexorable logic. Some unexpected consequences, some interesting distortions of long-celebrated icons are to be foreseen. The city and its architecture lose their symbols—no more monuments, no more axes, no more anthropomorphic symmetries, but instead fragmentation, parcellization, atomization, as well as the random superimposition of images that bear no relationship to one another, except through their collision. No wonder that some architectural projects sublimate the idea of *explosion.* A few architects do it in the form of drawings in which floor plans, beams, and walls seem to disintegrate in the darkness of outer space. Some even succeed in building those explosions and other accidents (by giving them the appearance of control—clients want control—but it's only a "simulation").

Hence the fascination for cinematic analogies: on the one hand, moving cranes and expressways and, on the other, montage techniques borrowed from film and video—frames and sequences, lap dissolves, fade-ins and fade-outs, jump cuts, and so forth.

One must remember that, initially, the sciences were about substance, about foundation: geology, physiology, physics, and gravity. And architecture was very much part of that concern, with its focus on solidity, firmness, structure, and hierarchy. Those foundations began to crumble in the twentieth century. Relativity, quantum theory, the uncertainty principle: this shakeup occurred not only in physics, as we know, but also in philosophy, the social sciences, and economics.

How then can architecture maintain some solidity, some degree of certainty? It seems impossible today—unless one decides that the accident or the explosion is to be called the rule, the new regulation, through a sort of philosophical inversion that considers the accident the norm and continuity the exception.

No more certainties, no more continuities. We hear that energy, as well as matter, is a discontinuous structure of points: punctum, quantum. Question: could the only certainty be the *point*?

The crises of determinism, or cause-and-effect relationships, and of continuity completely challenge recent architectural thought. Here, bear with me if I go through a rather tedious but quick recapitulation of "meaning" in architecture—without entering into a detailed discussion of Ferdinand de Saussure or Émile Benveniste. Ethnologists tell us that, in traditional symbolic relations, things have meanings. Quite often the symbolic value is separated from the utilitarian one. The Bauhaus tried to reconcile the two into a new functional duo of signifier and signified—a great synthesis. Moreover, the Bauhaus attempted to institute a "universal semanticization of the environment in which everything became the object of function and of signification" (Jean Baudrillard). This functionality, this synthesis of form and function, tried to turn the whole world into a homogeneous signifier, objectified as an element of signification: for every form, every signifier, there is an objective signified, a function. By focusing on denotation, it eliminated connotation.

Of course, this dominant discourse of rationality was bound to be attacked. At that time, it was by the surrealists, whose transgressions often relied on the ethics of functionalism, *a contrario.* In fact, some fixed, almost functionalist expectations were necessary to the surrealists, for they could only be unsettled through confrontation: the surreal set combining "the sewing machine and the umbrella on the dissecting table" only works because each of these objects represents a precise and unequivocal function.

The transgressed order of functionality that resulted reintroduced the order of the symbolic, now distorted and turned into a poetic phantasm. It liberated the object from its function, denounced the gap between subject and object, and encouraged free association. But such transgressions generally acted upon singular objects, while the world was becoming an environment of ever-increasing complex and abstract systems. The abstraction of the following years—whether expressionist or geometric—had its architectural equivalent. The endlessly repeated grids of skyscrapers were associated with a new zero-degree of meaning: perfect functionalism.

Fashion upset all that. It had always addressed issues of connotation: against fashion's unstable and ever-disappearing image, the stable and universal denotations of functionalism appeared particular and restrictive.

Partly fascinated by such connotations, partly longing for some long-lost traditional forms, architectural postmodernism in the seventies attempted to combine—to quote Charles Jencks—"modern techniques with traditional building, in order to communicate both with the public *and* with an elite" (hence "double-coding"). It was above all concerned with *codes*, with communicating some *message*, some *signified* (perhaps characterized by irony, parody, eclecticism). Architectural postmodernism was totally in line with the mission of architecture according to dominant history, which has been to invest shelter with a given meaning.

Ten years later, the illusion was already vanishing. The Doric orders made of painted plywood had begun to warp and peel. The instability, the ephemerality of both signifier and signified, form and function, form and meaning could only stress the obvious, what Jacques Lacan had pointed to years before: that there is no cause-and-effect relationship between signifier and signified, between word and intended concept. The signifier does not have to answer for its existence in the name of some hypothetical signification. As in literature and psychoanalysis, the architectural signifier does not represent the signified. Doric columns and neon pediments suggest too many interpretations to justify any single one. Again, there is no cause-and-effect relationship between an architectural sign and its possible interpretation. Between signifier and signified stands a barrier: the barrier of actual use. Never mind if this very room was once a fire station, then a furniture storage room, then a ritualistic

dance hall, and now a lecture hall (it has been all of these).
Each time, these uses distorted both signifier and signified.
Not only are linguistic signs arbitrary (as de Saussure showed
us long ago), but interpretation is itself open to constant
questioning. Every interpretation can be the object of interpretation, and that new interpretation can in turn be interpreted, until every interpretation erases the previous one.
The dominant history of architecture, which is a history of
the signified, has to be revised, at a time when there is no
longer a normative rule, a cause-and-effect relationship between a form and a function, between a signifier and its
signified: only a deregulation of meaning.

The deregulation of architecture began long
ago, at the end of the nineteenth century, with the world
fairs of London and Paris, where light metallic structures
radically changed the appearance of architectural solids. Suddenly, architecture was merely scaffolding supporting glass,
and it was discrediting the "solid," symbolic character of
masonry and stone. Human scale ceased to be an issue, as
the logic of industrial construction took over. Human proportions from the ages of classicism and humanism were
rapidly replaced by grids and modular systems, a superimposition of light and materials that were becoming increasingly immaterial—another form of deconstruction.

In the mid-seventies, nostalgic architects,
longing for meaning and tradition, applied sheetrock and
plywood cutouts to those scaffoldings, but the images they

were trying to provide were weak in comparison to the new scaffoldings of our time: the mediatized images of ephemeral representations.

"To represent construction or to construct representation" (Virilio): this is the new question of our time. As Albert Einstein said, "There is no scientific truth, only temporary representations, ever-accelerating sequences of representation." In fact, we are forced to go through a complete reconsideration of all concepts of figuration and representation: the constant storm of images (whether drawings, graphs, photographs, films, television, or computer-generated images) increasingly negates any attempt to restore the Renaissance ideal of the unity of reality and its representation. The concept of double-coding was the last and futile attempt to keep some of that ideal intact by establishing a new relation between communication and tradition. It is the word "tradition" that misled much of the architectural scene in the late seventies and made some aspects of architectural postmodernism what I think will soon appear as a short-lived avatar of history: a form of contextual eclecticism that has been recurrent throughout architectural history, with and without irony, allegory, and other parodies.

In any case, the problem is not a problem of images: gables and classical orders, however silly, are free to be consumed by whoever wishes to do so. But to pretend that these images could suggest new rules and regulations in architecture and urbanism by transcending modernism is simply misplaced.

There are no more rules and regulations. The current metropolitan deregulation caused by the dis-industrialization of European and American cities, by the collapse of zoning strategies, contradicts any attempt to develop new sets of regulating forces, however desirable it may be for some. The 1987 Wall Street "crash" and its relation to the economic deregulation that immediately preceded it is another illustration that an important change has taken place. Let me go back again to Virilio's argument. In the Middle Ages, society was self-regulated, auto-regulated. Regulation took place at its center. The prince of the city was the ruler; there was a direct cause-and-effect relationship between rules and everyday life, between the weight of masonry and the way that buildings were built.

In the industrial era, societies became artificially regulated. The power of economic and industrial forces took over by establishing a coherent structure throughout the whole territory: control was defined at the limits, at the edges of society. The relation between rules and everyday life ceased to be clear, and so large bureaucracies and administrators took over. Regulation was not at the center anymore but at the periphery. Abstract architecture used grids on its sheds International-style, before it discovered that one could decorate the same shed Multinational-style—regardless of what happened in them. Function, form, and meaning ceased to have any relationship to one another.

Today we have entered the age of deregulation, where control takes place *outside* of society, as in those computer programs that feed on one another endlessly in a form of autonomy, recalling the autonomy of language described by Michel Foucault. We witness the separation of people and language, the decentering of the subject. Or, we might say, the complete *decentering of society.*

Ex-centric, dis-integrated, dis-located, disjuncted, deconstructed, dismantled, disassociated, discontinuous, deregulated . . . de-, dis-, ex-. These are the prefixes of today. Not post-, neo-, or pre-.

Folie P6, Parc de la Villette, Paris, 1985.

Six Concepts   ▬

In an article published in January 1991 in *The New York Times,* Vincent Scully, a respected architectural critic and historian, stated that "the most important movement in architecture today is the revival of the vernacular and classical traditions and their reintegration into the mainstream of modern architecture in its fundamental aspect: the structure of communities, the building of towns." Professor Scully's words cannot easily be ignored, especially when, in

Delivered as a University Lecture at Columbia University in February 1991.

the same article, he pronounces the rest of the architectural profession to be in "a moment of supreme silliness that deconstructs and self-destructs."

I would like to pursue a short exploration of some of the issues that are addressed by those who, because they do not wish to perpetuate the revival of the vernacular and the classical, are now condemned to that "supreme silliness." I want to examine some of the concepts that govern the making of architecture and cities at this particular period—a period that cannot easily be recontained within the comforting fiction of an eighteenth-century village.

If we were to characterize our contemporary condition, we could say it is "after simulation," "postmediation." What do we do after everything has been relived at least once, after everything has been presented, re-presented, and re-re-presented? In order to elaborate on this, please allow me to briefly recapitulate our recent architectural past.

Much of architectural postmodernism was developed at a time of general reaction against what was perceived as the abstraction of modernism: abstraction because modernism's glass office buildings were "imageless" and cold like abstract painting. Abstraction too because, it was said, modern architects were elitist, detached, or "abstracted" from everyday life—from people and, above all, from the community that was not allowed to "participate" while zoning, highways, and high-rise housing (to quote Scully again) "destroyed the very fabric of our neighborhoods." Were Brasilia and Chandigarh beautiful or ugly, social or asocial, historical or ahistorical?

This reaction against the perception of modernity as the abstract reducer dates from the mid-1960s, whether through scholarly texts or through the first organized protests against the demolition of neighborhoods and landmark buildings in the name of progress, from New York's Pennsylvania Station to Paris's Les Halles. Among architects, it is certainly a book, Robert Venturi's *Complexity and Contradiction in Architecture*, published by The Museum of Modern Art in 1966, that triggered an extraordinary and widespread reappraisal of architectural priorities and values, suggesting that there was more to architecture than the ethereal, abstract formulation of a utopian ideal. Filled with examples that ranged from Borromini's work to "juxtapositions of expressways and existing buildings," Venturi's text concluded by praising "the vivid lessons of Pop Art," for pop art involved contradictions of scale and context "that should have awakened architects from their prim dreams of pure order."

Almost simultaneously, a new area of knowledge was developing that was to prove a formidable instrument in the hands of architects and critics who sought to restore meaning to what they had attacked as the zero degree of modernism. Semiology and linguistics invaded the architectural scene. Often greatly misunderstood, the work of Noam Chomsky, Umberto Eco, and Roland Barthes was to inform new architectural strategies of coding, so that ordinary people and scholars alike could finally decode multiple meanings pasted onto what nevertheless remained neutral sheds. While as early as 1968 Barthes, in one of his rare

ventures into urbanism and architecture, had concluded with
the impossibility of fixed meanings, postmodern architects
and critics developed a most unusual construct of a signifying
architecture in which building facades would convey a world
of allusions, quotations, and historical precedents.

Particular to these allusions is that they all
referred to a very narrow sector of architectural culture: first,
they dealt only with the *appearance* of architecture, with its
surface or image, never with its structure or use. Second, a
very restricted set of images was being proposed—Roman
palazzi, villas, and English vernacular buildings, or what
could be described as the Arcadian dreams of a conservative
middle class whose homogeneity of taste disproved the very
theories of heterogeneity that Barthes and Venturi seemed
to suggest. In passing, it should be added that for others who
were proposing a new formalist vocabulary instead, the same
situation often occurred. The talk was mostly about *image,*
about *surface;* structure and use were not mentioned. Indeed,
the industrial and metropolitan culture of our society was
notoriously absent. Rare were allusions to the megalopolis,
to factories, power stations, and other mechanical works that
had defined our culture for more than a century. In contrast,
we were treated to a constant set of images of a preindustrial
society—pre-airport, pre-supermarket, pre-computer, pre-
nuclear.

Of course, developers and builders were as
easily convinced by these "classical" architects as by preser-
vationists: the world of nostalgia, of comfort, of *geborgenheit*
would be a better world to live in, and more houses could be

sold. Despite recent interest in new forms of contemporary architecture, this preindustrial Arcadia constitutes the mainstream of architectural and political ideology in most of the built world. The more ideologically inclined among the apologists of revival argue that at the end of the twentieth century, after hundreds of years of industrial, technological, and social development, it is still possible to return to an earlier lifestyle, ignoring cars, computers, and the nuclear age. And, more important, ignoring the specific social and historical changes that took place during this time. These ideologists claim that the Arcadian "towns" now being developed on the model of holiday villages will, by virtue of their architecture, foster ideal communities where social values and respect for one another will replace difference, conflict, and urban interchange. This kind of community dream (shared by co-op boards and politicians alike) is ironic when proposed in a city like New York, where people move an average of every four years. However, it is symptomatic of a fantasy: that the village of our ancestors—one that we have never known—can be a model for generations to come.

But are modern versus classical or vernacular images really the issue? Pitched roofs against flat roofs? Is it really a key question? Of course not. I would claim that our contemporary condition affects historicists and modernists alike.

Part I

I have always been fascinated by the construction phase of two Manhattan buildings that were erected simultaneously and side-by-side on Madison Avenue in the Upper Fifties. These two skyscrapers, one designed for IBM and the other for AT&T, are almost identical in their steel structure, function, and office layout. The skins of both buildings are hung onto their structures using the same technique of lattice and clips. But here the similarities end. In the first case, the IBM building is clad with a slick, polished marble and glass facade, with abstract and minimalist detailing. In contrast, the AT&T building has a slightly articulated facade treatment with pink granite slabs cut to resemble Roman and Gothic stonework. The IBM building has a flat roof; the AT&T, a pediment. Until recently, the IBM building was seen as a symbol of a passé modernist era, the AT&T building as the heroic statement of the new historicist postmodernism that became the established corporate style of the 1980s. Both buildings are nearly identical in content, bulk, and use. Less than ten years later the same situation was repeated in Times Square, with a proposal for a so-called deconstructivist skin replacing a postmodern classical one. Such examples also apply to houses in East Hampton, Long Island where the designs of Robert A. M. Stern and Charles Gwathmey often serve the same programs, and sometimes the same clients. One architect is labeled a historicist, the other a modernist in their manufacture of fashionable images.

Such work on the surface can also be seen in building renovations, as in the Biltmore Hotel in New York, where a 1913 brick facade was replaced seventy-five years later by a more businesslike curtain wall. Almost simultaneously, the white tile facade of Columbia University's East Campus dormitories was being replaced by an imitation 1913 brick facade. This comment is *not* a value judgment: it has become a condition of our time. It should be noted that the administration and trustees of Columbia University agonized over what to do with the building when they found that the falling tiles could not be repaired or replaced, and that the alternative was to find $70 million to build a new dorm. No one is happy about the decision the university had to make—to change the skin—but if it is of any comfort, one can think of that shedding skin as a symptom of our contemporary condition, rather than as a result of faulty construction.

"The triumph of the superficial," as Stuart Ewen calls it in his recent book on the politics of style, *All Consuming Images,* is not a new phenomenon, but architects have yet to understand the consequences of this separation of structure and surface. Until the nineteenth century, architecture made use of load-bearing walls that held the building up. Although it was common to apply decorations of various styles to these surfaces, the walls performed a key structural function. Often there was a connection between the type of image used and the structure of the wall. By the 1830s the connection between image, structure, and construction method was gone. New construction methods employed an inner structural frame that supported the building. Whether in the form of "balloon frame" structures covered by a skin or of "structural frames" covered by curtain walls, these new building techniques meant that walls no longer played a structural role: they became increasingly ornamental. A multiplicity of styles became possible due to the development of prefabricated panels, ready to be shaped, painted, or printed to reflect any image, any period.

With the new disembodied skins, the roles of engineer and architect became increasingly separate: the engineer took care of the frame, the architect the skin. Architecture was becoming a matter of appearances: the skin could be Romanesque, Baroque, Victorian, "regionalist vernacular," and so on. This evolution of the interchangeability of surfaces coincided with new techniques of visual representation. Photography and the mass printing of decorative wallpapers further democratized the merchandising of surface treatments in architecture. Above all, photography increased the power of the image over any structure of substance.

We are talking about the nineteenth century, but things have intensified so much that the quantitative change has led to a qualitative leap. With photography, magazines, television, and buildings designed by fax, so-called superficiality has become the sign of our times. To quote Jean Baudrillard in "Transparency of Evil": ". . . things continue functioning when their idea has long disappeared from [them]. They continue to function with a total indifference to their own content. Paradoxically, they even function better this way."

Looked at in this matter, modernist buildings became "better" in the 1930s when social ideals began to prove illusive and finally vanished. By extension, are not Richard Meier's buildings today more "esthetic" than Le Corbusier's? A generalized form of estheticization has indeed taken place, conveyed by the media. Just as Stealth Bombers were estheticized on the televised Saudi Arabian sunset, just as sex is estheticized in advertising, so all of culture—and of course this includes architecture—is now estheticized, "xeroxized." Furthermore, the simultaneous presentation of these images leads to a reduction of history to simultaneous images: not only to those of the Gulf War interspersed with basketball games and advertisement but also to those of our architectural magazines and, ultimately, to those of our cities.

The media appetite for the consumption of architectural images is enormous. And one consequence of the shift of attention toward the surface has been that much of architectural history has become the printed image, the printed word (and their dissemination), and not the actual building. At the time of this writing, influential architectural personalities—Daniel Libeskind for example, or Wolf Prix, Zaha Hadid, or Rem Koolhaas—have built relatively little. Our generation of architects is the subject of countless articles, even though it is only infrequently given the power to build. Still, it dominates media information. The intensity of this information offensive, or what we might call "reality," is such that a single, objective reality is increasingly difficult to conceive. We are familiar with Nietzsche's aphorism in *Twilight of the Idols:* "The real world, finally, will become a fiction." Inevitably, architecture and its perception will become like another object of contemporary reality.

Eclectic classicism, rationalism, neomodernism, deconstructivism, critical regionalism, green architecture, or, in the art world, neo-geo, new expressionism, new abstraction, or figuration—all of them *coexist* and increasingly provoke in us a profound indifference: indifference to difference. From *The New York Times* to *Vanity Fair,* from *P/A* and *A.D.* to *Assemblage,* we see a multiple reality that is increasingly based on a constant oscillation between trends, theories, schools, movements, and waves. The question is: why *oppose* this mediated world? Should it be in the name of some solid, unified reality? Should we once again long for a coherent *Gesamtkunstwerk*? But today, the project of the early twentieth-century appears as a wish to restore a society in which every element is in a fixed hierarchical relationship with every other—a world of order, certainty, and permanence.

Indeed, if most of architecture has become surface, applied decoration, superficiality, paper architecture (or to use Venturi's celebrated expression, "decorated shed"), what distinguishes architecture from other forms of billboard design: or, more ambitiously, what distinguishes architecture from editions, layouts, graphics? If the so-called contextualisms and typological historicisms are nothing but a set of opportune disguises applied to a ready-made formula—in other words, a skin on a frame that respects or disrupts the bulk of the adjacent buildings—then how can architecture remain a means by which society explores new territories, develops new knowledge?

Part II

Concept I: Technologies of Defamiliarization In recent years, small pockets of resistance began to form as architects in various parts of the world—England, Austria, the United States, Japan (for the most part, in advanced postindustrial cultures)—started to take advantage of this condition of fragmentation and superficiality and to turn it against itself. If the prevalent ideology was one of familiarity—familiarity with known images, derived from 1920s modernism or eighteenth-century classicism—maybe one's role was to *defamiliarize*. If the new, mediated world echoed and reinforced our dismantled reality, maybe, just maybe, one should take advantage of such dismantling, *celebrate fragmentation* by *celebrating the culture of differences*, by accelerating and intensifying the loss of certainty, of center, of history.

In culture in general, the world of communication in the last twenty years has certainly helped the expression of a multiplicity of new angles on the canonic story, airing the views of women, immigrants, gays, minorities, and various non-Western identities who never sat comfortably within the supposed community. In architecture in particular, the notion of defamiliarization was a clear tool. If the design of windows only reflects the superficiality of the

North-South Gallery, Parc de la Villette, Paris, 1985.

Inhabited bridges, Lausanne, 1988.

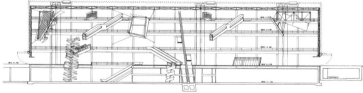

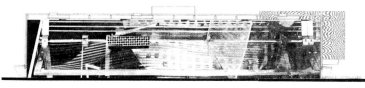

ZKM, Karlsruhe, Germany, 1988.

Le Fresnoy, Center for Art and Media, Tourcoing, France, 1991.

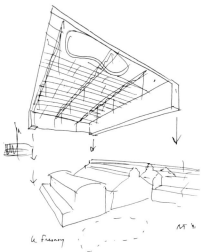

Le Fresnoy   NT 91

Disjunction

Glass video gallery, Groningen, the Netherlands, 1988.

Bibliothèque de France, Paris, 1988.

Disjunction

Le Fresnoy, Center for Art and Media, Tourcoing, France, 1991.

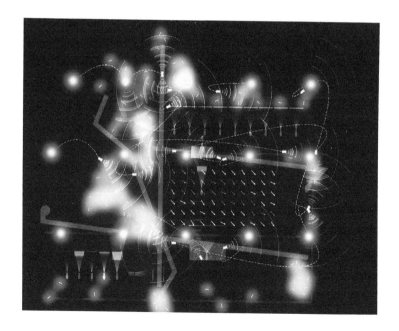

skin's decoration, we might very well start to look for a way to do without windows. If the design of pillars reflects the conventionality of a supporting frame, maybe we might get rid of pillars altogether.

Although the architects concerned might not profess an inclination toward the exploration of new technologies, such work usually took advantage of contemporary technological developments. Interestingly, the specific technologies—air conditioning, or the construction of lightweight structures, or computer modes of calculation—have yet to be theorized in architectural culture. I stress this because other technological advances, such as the invention of the elevator or the nineteenth-century development of steel construction, have been the subject of countless studies by historians, but very little such work exists in terms of contemporary technologies because these technologies do not necessarily produce historical forms.

I take this detour through technology because technology is inextricably linked to our contemporary condition: to say that society is now about media and mediation makes us aware that the direction taken by technology is less the domination of nature through technology than the development of information and the construction of the world as a set of images. Architects must again understand and take advantage of the use of such new technologies. In the words of the French writer, philosopher, and architect Paul Virilio, "we are not dealing anymore with the technology of construction, but with the construction of technology."

Concept II: The Mediated "Metropolitan" Shock That constant flickering of images fascinates us, much as it fascinated Walter Benjamin in *The Work of Art in the Age of Mechanical Reproduction.* I hate to cite such a "classic," but Gianni Vattimo's recent analysis of the text has indicated aspects that are illustrative of our contemporary condition. When Benjamin discussed the reproducibility of images, he pointed out that the loss of their exchange value, their "aura," made them interchangeable, and that in an age of pure information the only thing that counted was the "shock"—the shock of images, their surprise factor. This shock factor was what allowed an image to stand out: moreover, it was also characteristic of our contemporary condition and of the dangers of life in the modern metropolis. These dangers resulted in constant anxiety about finding oneself in a world in which everything was insignificant and gratuitous. The experience of such anxiety was an experience of defamiliarization, of *Un-zu-hause-sein,* of *Unheimlichkeit,* of the uncanny.

In many ways, the esthetic experience, according to Benjamin, consisted of keeping defamiliarization alive, as contrasted to its opposite—familiarization, security, *Geborgenheit.* I would like to point out that Benjamin's analysis corresponds exactly to the historical and philosophical dilemma of architecture. Is the experience of architecture something that is meant to defamiliarize—let's say, a form of "art"—or, on the contrary, is it something that is meant to be comforting, *heimlich,* homely—something that protects? Here, of course, one recognizes the constant opposition between those who see architecture and our cities as places of experience and experiment, as exciting reflections of contemporary society—those who like "things that go bump in the night," that deconstruct and self-destruct—and those who see the role of architecture as refamiliarization, contextualization, insertion—in other words, those who describe themselves as historicists, contextualists, and postmodernists, since postmodernism in architecture now has a definitely classicist and historicist connotation.

The general public will almost always stand behind the traditionalists. In the public eye, architecture is about comfort, about shelter, about bricks and mortar. However, for those for whom architecture is not necessarily about comfort and *Geborgenheit*, but is also about advancing society and its development, the device of shock may be an indispensable tool. Cities like New York, despite—or maybe because of—its homeless and two thousand murders a year become the postindustrial equivalent of Georg Simmel's preindustrial *Grosstadt* that so fascinated and horrified Benjamin. Architecture in the megalopolis may be more about finding unfamiliar solutions to problems than about the quieting, comforting solutions of the establishment community.

Recently, we have seen important new research on cities in which the fragmentation and dislocation produced by the scaleless juxtaposition of highways, shopping centers, high-rise buildings, and small houses is seen as a positive sign of the vitality of urban culture. As opposed to nostalgic attempts to restore an impossible continuity of streets and plazas, this research implies making an event out of urban shock, intensifying and accelerating urban experience through clash and disjunction.

Let us return to the media. In our era of reproduction, we have seen how the conventional construction techniques of frame and skin correspond to the superficiality and precariousness of media culture, and how a constant expansion of change was necessary to satisfy the often banal needs of the media. We have also seen that to endorse this logic means that any work is interchangeable with any other, just as we accelerate the shedding of the skin of a dormitory and replace it with another. We have also seen that the shock goes against the nostalgia of permanence or authority, whether it is in culture in general or architecture in particular. Over fifty years after the publication of Benjamin's text, we may have to say that shock is still all we have left to communicate in a time of generalized information. In a world heavily influenced by the media, this relentless need for change is not necessarily to be understood as negative. The increase in change and superficiality also means a weakening of architecture as a form of domination, power, and authority, as it historically has been in the last six thousand years.

Concept III: De-structuring This "weakening" of architecture, this altered relationship between structure and image, structure and skin, is interesting to examine in the light of a debate that has resurfaced recently in architectural circles—namely, structure versus ornament. Since the Renaissance, architectural theory has always distinguished between structure and ornament and has set forth the hierarchy between them. To quote Leon Battista Alberti: "Ornament has the character of something attached or additional." Ornament is meant to be additive; it must not challenge or weaken the structure.

But what does this hierarchy mean today, when the structure often remains the same—an endlessly repetitive and neutralized grid? In the majority of construction in this country today, structural practice is rigorously similar in concept: a basic frame of wood, steel, or concrete. As noted earlier, the decision whether to construct the frame from any of these materials is often left to the engineers and economists rather than to the architect. The architect is not meant to question structure. The structure *must* stand firm. After all, what would happen to insurance premiums (and to reputations) if the building collapsed? The result is too often a refusal to question structure. The structure must be stable, otherwise the edifice collapses—the edifice, that is, both the building and the entire edifice of thought. For in comparison to science or philosophy, architecture rarely questions its foundations.

The result of these "habits of mind" in architecture is that the structure of a building is not supposed to be questioned anymore than are the mechanics of a projector when watching a movie or the hardware of a television set when viewing images on its screen. Social critics regularly question the image yet rarely question the apparatus, the frame. Still, for over a century, and especially in the past twenty years, we have seen the beginning of such questioning. Contemporary philosophy has touched upon this relationship between frame and image—here the frame is seen as the structure, the armature, and the image as the ornament. Jacques Derrida's *Parergon* turns such questioning between frame and image into a theme. Although it might be argued that the frame of a painting does not quite equate to the frame of a building—one being exterior or "hors d'oeuvre" and the other interior—I would maintain that this is only a *superficial* objection. Traditionally, both frame and structure perform the same function of "holding it together."

Concept IV: Superimposition This questioning of structure led to a particular side of contemporary architectural debate, namely deconstruction. From the beginning, the polemics of deconstruction, together with much of poststructuralist thought, interested a small number of architects because it seemed to question the very principles of *Geborgenheit* that the postmodernist mainstream was trying to promote. When I first met Jacques Derrida in order to try to convince him to confront his own work with architecture, he asked me, "But how could an architect be interested in deconstruction? After all, deconstruction is anti-form, anti-hierarchy, anti-structure, the opposite of all that architecture stands for." "Precisely for this reason," I replied.

As years went by, the multiple interpretations that multiple architects gave to deconstruction became more multiple than deconstruction's theory of multiple readings could ever have hoped. For one architect it had to do with dissimulation; for another, with fragmentation; for yet another, with displacement. Again, to quote Nietzsche: "There are no facts, only an infinity of interpretations." And very soon, maybe due to the fact that many architects shared the same dislike for the *Geborgenheit* of the "historicist postmodernists" and the same fascination for the early twentieth-century avant-garde, *deconstructivism* was born—and immediately called a "style"—precisely what these architects had been trying to avoid. Any interest in poststructuralist thought and deconstruction stemmed from the fact that they challenged the idea of a single unified set of images, the idea of certainty, and of course, the idea of an identifiable language.

Theoretical architects—as they were called—wanted to confront the binary oppositions of traditional architecture: namely, form versus function, or abstraction versus figuration. However, they also wanted to challenge the implied hierarchies hidden in these dualities, such as, "form *follows* function," and "ornament is subservient to structure." This repudiation of hierarchy led to a fascination with complex images that were simultaneously "both" and "neither/nor"—images that were the overlap or the superimposition of many other images. Superimposition became a key device. This can be seen in my own work. In *The Manhattan Transcripts* (1981) or *The Screenplays* (1977), the devices used in the first episodes were borrowed from film theory and the *nouveau roman*. In the *Transcripts* the distinction between structure (or frame), form (or space), event (or function), body (or movement), and fiction (or narrative) was systematically blurred through superimposition, collision, distortion, fragmentation, and so forth. We find superimposition used quite remarkably in Peter Eisenman's work, where the overlays for his *Romeo and Juliet* project pushed literary and philosophical parallels to extremes. These different realities challenged any single interpretation, constantly trying to problematize the architectural object, crossing boundaries between film, literature, and architecture. ("Was it a play or was it a piece of architecture?")

Much of this work benefited from the environment of the universities and the art scene—its galleries and publications—where the crossover among different fields allowed architects to blur the distinctions between genres, constantly questioning the discipline of architecture and its hierarchies of form. Yet if I was to examine both my own work of this time and that of my colleagues, I would say that both grew out of a *critique* of architecture, of the nature of architecture. It dismantled concepts and became a remarkable conceptual tool, but it could not address the one thing that makes the work of architects ultimately different from the work of philosophers: *materiality.*

Just as there is a logic of words or of drawings, there is a logic of materials, and they are not the same. And however much they are subverted, something ultimately resists. *Ceci n'est pas une pipe.* A word is not a concrete block. The concept of dog does not bark. To quote Gilles Deleuze, "The concepts of film are not given in film." When metaphors and catachreses are turned into buildings, they generally turn into plywood or papier mâché stage sets: the ornament again. Sheetrock columns that do not touch the ground are not structural, they are ornament. Yes, fiction and narrative fascinated many architects, perhaps because, our enemies might say, we knew more about books than about buildings.

I do not have the time to dwell upon an interesting difference between the two interpretations of the role of fiction in architecture: one, the so-called historicist postmodernist allegiance, the other, the so-called deconstructivist neomodernist allegiance (not my labels). Although both stemmed from early interests in linguistics and semiology, the first group saw fiction and narrative as part of the realm of metaphors, of a new *architecture parlante*, of *form*, while the second group saw fiction and scenarios as analogues for programs and *function*.

I would like to concentrate on that second view. Rather than manipulating the formal properties of architecture, we might look into what really happens inside buildings and cities: the function, the program, the properly *historical* dimension of architecture. Roland Barthes's *Structural Analysis of Narratives* was fascinating in this respect, for it could be directly transposed both in spatial and programmatic sequence. The same could be said of much of Sergei Eisenstein's theory of film montage.

Concept V: Crossprogramming Architecture has always been as much about the event that takes place in a space as about the space itself. The Columbia University Rotunda has been a library; it has been used as a banquet hall; it is often the site of university lectures; someday it could fulfill the needs for an athletic facility at the university. What a wonderful swimming pool the Rotunda would be! You may think I'm being facetious, but in today's world where railway stations become museums and churches become nightclubs, a point is being made: the complete interchangeability of form and function, the loss of traditional, canonic cause-and-effect relationships as sanctified by modernism. Function does not follow form, form does not follow function—or fiction for that matter—however, they certainly interact. Diving into this great blue Rotunda pool—a part of the *shock.*

If shock can no longer be produced by the succession and juxtaposition of facades and lobbies, maybe it can be produced by the juxtaposition of events that take place behind these facades in these spaces. If "the respective contamination of all categories, the constant substitutions, the confusion of genres"—as described by critics of the right and left alike from Andreas Huyssens to Jean Baudrillard— is the new direction of our times, it may well be used to one's advantage, to the advantage of a general rejuvenation of architecture. If architecture is both concept and experience, space and use, structure and superficial image—nonhierarchically—then architecture should cease to separate these categories and instead merge them into unprecedented combinations of programs and spaces. "Crossprogramming," "transprogramming," "disprogramming": I have elaborated on these concepts elsewhere, suggesting the displacement and mutual contamination of terms.

Concept VI: Events: The Turning Point   My own work in the 1970s constantly reiterated that there was no architecture without event, no architecture without action, without activities, without functions. Architecture was seen as the combination of spaces, events, and movements without any hierarchy or precedence among these concepts. The hierarchical cause-and-effect relationship between function and form is one of the great certainties of architectural thinking— the one that lies behind that reassuring *idée reçue* of community life that tells us that we live in houses "designed to answer to our needs," or in cities planned as machines to live in. *Geborgenheit* connotations of this notion go against both the real "pleasure" of architecture, in its unexpected combinations of terms, and the reality of contemporary urban life in its most stimulating, unsettling directions. Hence, in works like *The Manhattan Transcripts,* the definition of architecture could not be form or walls but had to be the combination of heterogeneous and incompatible terms.

The insertion of the terms *event* and *movement* was influenced by Situationist discourse and by the '68 era. *Les événements,* as they were called, were not only events in action but also in thought. Erecting a barricade (function) in a Paris street (form) is not quite equivalent to being a *flaneur* (function) in that same street (form). Dining (function) in the Rotunda (form) is not quite equivalent to reading or swimming in it. Here all hierarchical relationships between form and function cease to exist. This unlikely combination of events and spaces was charged with subversive capabilities, for it challenged both the function and the space. Such confrontation parallels the Surrealists' meeting of a sewing machine and an umbrella on a dissecting table or, closer to us, Rem Koolhaas's description of the Downtown Athletic Club: "Eating oysters with boxing gloves, naked, on the nth floor."

We find it today in Tokyo, with multiple programs scattered throughout the floors of high-rise buildings: a department store, a museum, a health club, and a railway station, with putting greens on the roof. And we will find it in the programs of the future, where airports are simultaneously amusement arcades, athletic facilities, cinemas, and so on. Regardless of whether they are the result of chance combinations or are due to the pressure of ever-rising land prices, such noncausal relationships between form and function or space and action go beyond poetic confrontations of unlikely bedfellows. Michel Foucault, as cited in a book by John Rajchman, expanded the use of the term *event* in a manner that went beyond the single action or activity and spoke of "events of thought." For Foucault, an event is not simply a logical sequence of words or actions but rather "the moment of erosion, collapse, questioning, or problematization of the very assumptions of the setting within which a drama may take place—occasioning the chance or possibility of another, different setting." The event here is seen as a *turning point*—not an origin or an end—as opposed to such propositions as form follows function. I would like to propose that the future of architecture lies in the construction of such events.

Just as important is the spatialization that goes with the event. Such a concept is quite different from the project of the modern movement, which sought the affirmation of certainties in a unified utopia as opposed to our current questioning of multiple, fragmented, dislocated terrains.

A few years later, in an essay about the *folies* of the Parc de la Villette, Jacques Derrida expanded on the definition of *event*, calling it "the emergence of a disparate multiplicity." I had constantly insisted, in our discussions and elsewhere, that these points called *folies* were points of activities, of programs, of events. Derrida elaborated on this concept, proposing the possibility of an "architecture of the event" that would "eventualize," or open up that which, in our history or tradition, is understood to be fixed, essential, monumental. He had also suggested earlier that the word "event" shared roots with "invention," hence the notion of the event, of the action-in-space, of the turning point, the invention. I would like to associate it with the notion of shock, a shock that in order to be effective in our mediated culture, in our culture of images, must go beyond Walter Benjamin's definition and *combine the idea of function or action with that of image.* Indeed, architecture finds itself in a unique situation: it is the only discipline that by definition combines concept and experience, image and use, image and structure. Philosophers can write, mathematicians can develop virtual spaces, but architects are the only ones who are the prisoners of that hybrid art, where the image hardly ever exists without a combined activity.

It is my contention that far from being a field suffering from the incapability of questioning its structures and foundations, it is the field where the greatest discoveries will take place in the next century. The very heterogeneity of the definition of architecture—space, action, and movement—makes it into that *event,* that place of shock, or that place of the invention of ourselves. The event is the place where the rethinking and reformulation of the different elements of architecture, many of which have resulted in or added to contemporary social inequities, may lead to their solution. By definition, it is the place of the combination of differences.

This will not happen by imitating the past and eighteenth-century ornaments. It also will not happen by simply commenting, through design, on the various dislocations and uncertainties of our contemporary condition. I do not believe it is possible, nor does it make sense, to design buildings that *formally* attempt to blur traditional structures, that is, that display forms that lie somewhere between abstraction and figuration, or between structure and ornament, or that are cut up and dislocated for esthetic reasons. Architecture is not an illustrative art; it does not illustrate theories. (I do not believe you can design deconstruction.) You cannot design a new definition of cities and their architecture. But one may be able to design the conditions that will make it possible for this nonhierarchical, nontraditional society to happen. By understanding the nature of our contemporary circumstances and the media processes that accompany them, architects possess the possibility of constructing conditions that will create a new city and new relationships between spaces and events.

Architecture is not about the conditions of design but about the design of conditions that will dislocate the most traditional and regressive aspects of our society and simultaneously reorganize these elements in the most liberating way, so that our experience becomes the experience of events organized and strategized through architecture. Strategy is a key word in architecture today. No more masterplans, no more locating in a fixed place, but a new heterotopia. This is what our cities must strive toward and what we architects must help them to achieve by intensifying the rich collision of events and spaces. Tokyo and New York only appear chaotic. Instead, they mark the appearance of a new urban structure, a new urbanity. Their confrontations and combinations of elements may provide us with the event, the shock, that I hope will make the architecture of our cities a turning point in culture and society.

Notes

The Architectural Paradox

1.   For these issues, see the interpretation offered by Henri Lefèbvre in *La production de l'espace*, (Paris: Editions Anthrapos, 1973), and the texts of Castells and Utopie. See also Bernard Tschumi, "Flashback," on the politics of space, in *Architectural Design*, October–November 1975.

2.   Friedrich Hegel, *The Philosophy of Fine Art*, vol. 1 (London: G. Bell and Sons, Ltd, 1920).

3.   Etienne-Louis Boullée, *Essai sur l'Art*, ed. Perouse de Montclos (Paris: Herman, 1968).

4.   On the ideological crisis of architecture and the emergence of radical architecture, see Germano Celant (quoted here) in *The New Italian Landscape* (New York: Museum of Modern Art, 1972), 320.

5.   Originated in Florence from 1963 to 1971 by groups such as Superstudio, Archizoom, UFO, and so forth, radical architecture explored the destruction of culture and its artifacts. "The ultimate end of modern architecture is the elimination of architecture altogether" (Archizoom Associates).

6.   One of the first and most significant events of rational architecture was the XV Milan Triennale, organized by Aldo Rossi, whose catalogue, edited by Franco Angeli, bore the title of *Architettura Razionale* (Milan: F. Angeli, 1973).

7.   "The return to language is a proof of failure. It is necessary to examine to what degree such a failure is due to the intrinsic character of the architectural discipline and to what degree it is due to a still unresolved ambiguity." Manfredo Tafuri, *Oppositions 3*, May 1974, where the author develops a historical critique of traditional approaches to theory and shifts from a central focus on the criticism of architecture to the criticism of ideology.

8.   Denis Hollier, *La Prise de la Concorde* (Paris: Gallimard, 1974), the reading of which suggested the opposition between the labyrinth and the pyramid. See also Georges Bataille, *Eroticism* (London: Calder, 1962) and "L'Expérience Intérieure," in *Oeuvres Complètes* (Paris: Gallimard, 1971).

9.   Bernard Tschumi, "Fireworks," 1974, extract from *A Space: A Thousand Words* (London: Royal College of Art Gallery, 1975) "Yes, just as all the erotic forces contained in your movement have been consumed for nothing, architecture must be conceived, erected and burned in vain. The greatest architecture of all is the fireworker's: it perfectly shows the gratuitous consumption of pleasure."

10.   B. Spinoza (1622–1677), quoted by Henri Lefèbvre in conversation with the author, Paris, 1972.

Architecture and Transgression

1.   London, 1975. With Peter Eisenman, RoseLee Goldberg, Peter Cook, Colin Rowe, John Stezaker, Bernard Tschumi, Cedric Price, Will Alsop, Charles Jencks, and Joseph Rykwert, among others.

2.   Cf. G. W. F. Hegel, *The Philosophy of Fine Art,* vol. 1 (London: G. Bell and Sons, Ltd, 1920).

3.   See also such magazines as *Casabella* and *Architectural Design* for their documentation of the work of Superstudio, Archizoom, Hans Hollein, Walter Pichler, Raimund Abraham, and so forth.

4.   Cf. *Architettura Razionale,* (Milan: Franco Angeli, 1973).

5.   Cf. *A Space: A Thousand Words* (London: Royal College of Art Gallery, 1975); *The Chronicle of Space,* documenting student work done in the Diploma School of the Architectural Association, London, from 1974–1975; the "Real Space" conference at the Architectural Association with Germano Celant, Daniel Buren, Brian Eno, and others.

6.   It is not necessary to expatiate at length on the twentieth-century precedents. Suffice it to say that current discourse seems to fluctuate between the 1910 German aesthetic overtones of the *Raumempfindung* theory, whereby space is to be "felt" as some-

thing affecting the inner nature of man by a symbolic *Einfühlung*, and one that echoes Oskar Schlemmer's work at the Bauhaus, whereby space was not only the medium of experience but also the materialization of theory.

7.   This infinite tension between the two mirrors constitutes a void. As Oscar Wilde once pointed out, in order to defend any paradox, the wit depends on *memory*. By absorbing and reflecting all information, the mirrors—and the mind—become a wheel, a sort of circular retrieval system. In architecture, between the mirrors of ideal space and real space, the same thing happens. Long proscribed in an amnesic world where only progress and technological advance count, architectural memory returns. Cf. Antoine Grumbach, "L'Architecture et l'Evidente Nécessité de la Mémoire," *L'Art Vivant*, no. 56, January 1975.

8.   I discuss here only the resolution of the paradox in terms of a space *outside* the "subject." The argument could indeed be extended to the unqualifiable pleasure of drawing and to what could be called the "experience of concepts." Tracing Chinese ideograms, for example, means a double pleasure: for the experience of drawing reveals itself as a praxis of the sign, as a sensitive materiality with meaning. While with the paradox, it is tempting to try to uncover the mode of inscription of architectural concepts upon the unconscious. Especially if we admit that there is libido in all human activities, we may also consider that some architectural concepts are the expression of a sublimated model. See Daniel Sibony's article in *Psychanalyse et Sémiotique*, 10/18 (Paris: Collection Tel Quel, 1975).

9.   Too little research has been done on the relationship between architectonic concepts and the sensory experience of space:

"Those who negate sensations, who negate direct experience, who negate personal participation in a praxis which is aimed at transforming reality, are not materialists." (Mao Tse Tung, *Four Philosophical Essays*. Peking: 1967).

10.   Le Corbusier, *Vers Une Architecture* (Paris: L'Esprit Nouveau, 1928). One chapter is entitled "Architecture et Transgression." Not surprisingly, Le Corbusier's interpretation differs considerably from Bataille's and from the one discussed in my text.

11.   Ibid.

12.   Ibid.

13.   Georges Bataille, *Eroticism* (London: Calder, 1962).

Architecture and Limits

1.   *Oxford English Dictionary*, "to define."

2.   Ibid., "to limit."

3.   *Oxford English Dictionary.*

4.   J. Guadet, *Eléments et théorie de l'architecture.* Paris: 1909.

5.   Such projects began to emerge during the past decade, and range from Superstudio's *Ideal Cities* to John Hejduk's *Thirteen Towers of Canareggio.*

Sequences

1.   Bernard Tschumi, *The Manhattan Transcripts* (New York/London: St. Martin's Press/Academy Editions, 1981).

2. Roland Barthes, "Structural Analysis of Narratives," in *Image-Music-Text* (London: Fontana, 1977).

3. Luigi Moretti, "Structures and Sequences of Space," *Oppositions 4* (New York: Wittenborn Art Books, 1974).

4. *Oxford English Dictionary.*

Madness and the Combinative

1. *Folie* means "madness" in French, and although it also refers to small constructions hidden by dense foliage, its meaning—even applied to the built object—differs considerably from that of the English word "folly": "The name generally given to these dwellings by the eighteenth century was "little houses," not because they were small, but from a play on words deriving from popular humor. The idea of the *folie* was obviously associated with madness, and at that time lunatics were confined in the Hôpital des Petits Maisons or Little Houses—not the first instance, perhaps, nor the last, of a Parisian pun." From Michel Gallet, *Paris Domestic Architecture of the 18th Century* (London: Barrie and Jenkins, 1972).

2. Jacques Lacan, "Encore," *Séminaire,* Livre XX. Unless otherwise noted, all translations from the French in this text are by the author.

3. Ibid.

4. Jacques Lacan, "Les Ecrits Techniques de Freud," *Séminaire,* Livre I.

5. G. Pankov, "L'image du corps et objet transitionnel," *Revue Française de Psychanalyse* no. 2, 1976.

6.   It should be recalled here, that, after Lacan, psychoanalysis does not have as its goal curing patients, and that if people in analysis do get better, it is only a welcome side effect. The same applies to architecture. To make buildings that work and make people happy is not to goal of architecture but, of course, a welcome side effect.

7.   R. Bidault, "Approche du schizophrène en milieu institutionnel," *La Folie* 1, 10/18, 1977.

8.   Martin Heidegger, Questions IV, *Les Séminaires.*

9.   Bernard Tschumi, *The Manhattan Transcripts* (New York/London: St. Martin's Press/Academy Editions, 1981).

10.   Roland Barthes, *Sade, Fourier, Loyola,* trans. Richard Miller (New York: Hill and Wang, 1976).

11.   Gérard Genette, *Palimpsestes* (Paris: Editions du Seuil, 1982).

12.   One can extend this combination to the psychological level. In the preface to Diogenes Casares's *Invention of Morel,* Jorge Luis Borges notes that "the Russians and the disciples of the Russians have demonstrated *ad nauseum* that nothing is impossible: Suicides by excess of happiness, assassinations by charity, lovers who adore each other so to split up forever, traitors by love or humility . . . Such total freedom leads to total disorder."

13.   Tschumi, op. cit.

14.   Genette, op. cit.

Bernard Tschumi, Fireworks for La Villette, Paris, 1991.

PHASE III
4ème minute : Superposition , Points, Lignes, Surfaces

rythme: toutes les 7 secondes

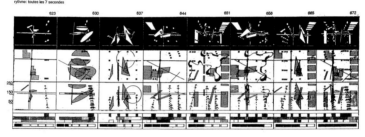